Contents

Foreword	3
About this booklet	5

About science in the National Curriculum

The structure of the National Curriculum	6
Learning across the National Curriculum	8

The programmes of study for science

A common structure and design for all subjects	12
The importance of science	15
Key stage 1	16
Key stage 2	21
Key stage 3	28
Key stage 4 single	37
Key stage 4 double	46

General teaching requirements

Inclusion: providing effective learning opportunities for all pupils	60
Use of language across the curriculum	69
Use of information and communication technology across the curriculum	70
Health and safety	71

The attainment targets for science

	73

Foreword

The National Curriculum lies at the heart of our policies to raise standards. It sets out a clear, full and statutory entitlement to learning for all pupils. It determines the content of what will be taught, and sets attainment targets for learning. It also determines how performance will be assessed and reported. An effective National Curriculum therefore gives teachers, pupils, parents, employers and their wider community a clear and shared understanding of the skills and knowledge that young people will gain at school. It allows schools to meet the individual learning needs of pupils and to develop a distinctive character and ethos rooted in their local communities. And it provides a framework within which all partners in education can support young people on the road to further learning.

Getting the National Curriculum right presents difficult choices and balances. It must be robust enough to define and defend the core of knowledge and cultural experience which is the entitlement of every pupil, and at the same time flexible enough to give teachers the scope to build their teaching around it in ways which will enhance its delivery to their pupils.

The focus of this National Curriculum, together with the wider school curriculum, is therefore to ensure that pupils develop from an early age the essential literacy and numeracy skills they need to learn; to provide them with a guaranteed, full and rounded entitlement to learning; to foster their creativity; and to give teachers discretion to find the best ways to inspire in their pupils a joy and commitment to learning that will last a lifetime.

An entitlement to learning must be an entitlement for all pupils. This National Curriculum includes for the first time a detailed, overarching statement on inclusion which makes clear the principles schools must follow in their teaching right across the curriculum, to ensure that all pupils have the chance to succeed, whatever their individual needs and the potential barriers to their learning may be.

Equality of opportunity is one of a broad set of common values and purposes which underpin the school curriculum and the work of schools. These also include a commitment to valuing ourselves, our families and other relationships, the wider groups to which we belong, the diversity in our society and the environment in which we live. Until now, ours was one of the few national curricula not to have a statement of rationale setting out the fundamental principles underlying the curriculum. The handbooks for primary and secondary teachers include for the first time such a statement.

This is also the first National Curriculum in England to include citizenship, from September 2002, as part of the statutory curriculum for secondary schools. Education in citizenship and democracy will provide coherence in the way in which all pupils are helped to develop a full understanding of their roles and responsibilities as citizens in a modern democracy. It will play an important role, alongside other aspects of the curriculum and school life, in helping pupils to deal with difficult moral and social questions that arise in their lives and in society. The handbooks also provide for the first time a national framework for the teaching of personal, social and health education. Both elements reflect the fact that education is also about helping pupils to develop the knowledge, skills and understanding they need to live confident, healthy, independent lives, as individuals, parents, workers and members of society.

Rt Hon David Blunkett
Secretary of State for Education
and Employment

Sir William Stubbs
Chairman, Qualifications
and Curriculum Authority

About this booklet

This booklet:

- sets out the legal requirements of the National Curriculum in England for science
- provides information to help teachers implement science in their schools.

It has been written for coordinators, subject leaders and those who teach science, and is one of a series of separate booklets for each National Curriculum subject.

The National Curriculum for pupils aged five to 11 is set out in the handbook for primary teachers. The National Curriculum for pupils aged 11 to 16 is set out in the handbook for secondary teachers.

All these publications, and materials that support the teaching, learning and assessment of science, can be found on the National Curriculum web site at www.nc.uk.net.

About science in the National Curriculum

The structure of the National Curriculum

The programmes of study[1] set out what pupils should be taught, and the attainment targets set out the expected standards of pupils' performance. It is for schools to choose how they organise their school curriculum to include the programmes of study for science.

The programmes of study

The programmes of study set out what pupils should be taught in science at key stages 1, 2, 3 and 4 and provide the basis for planning schemes of work. When planning, schools should also consider the general teaching requirements for inclusion, use of language, use of information and communication technology, and health and safety that apply across the programmes of study.

The **Knowledge, skills and understanding** in each programme of study identify the four areas of science that pupils study:

- scientific enquiry
- life processes and living things
- materials and their properties
- physical processes.

Teaching should ensure that scientific enquiry is taught through contexts taken from the sections on life processes and living things, materials and their properties and physical processes.

The **Breadth of study** identifies contexts in which science should be taught, makes clear that technological applications should be studied, and identifies what should be taught about communication and health and safety in science.

Schools may find the DfEE/QCA exemplar schemes of work at key stages 1, 2 and 3 helpful to show how the programmes of study and attainment targets can be translated into practical, manageable teaching plans.

Science at key stage 4

There are two programmes of study at key stage 4 – single science and double science. Pupils may be taught either the single or the double science programme of study. The requirements of either option would also be met by pupils taking GCSE courses in all three of the separate sciences of biology, chemistry and physics. The Government firmly believes that double science or the three separate sciences should be taken by the great majority of pupils. Single science is intended for a minority of pupils who have good reason to spend more time on other subjects.

---

[1] The Education Act 1996, section 353b, defines a programme of study as the 'matters, skills and processes' that should be taught to pupils of different abilities and maturities during the key stage.

Attainment targets and level descriptions

The attainment targets for science set out the 'knowledge, skills and understanding that pupils of different abilities and maturities are expected to have by the end of each key stage'[2]. Attainment targets consist of eight level descriptions of increasing difficulty, plus a description for exceptional performance above level 8. Each level description describes the types and range of performance that pupils working at that level should characteristically demonstrate.

In science, the level descriptions indicate progression in the knowledge, skills and understanding set out in the four main sections of the programme of study: scientific enquiry, life processes and living things, materials and their properties and physical processes. The examples given in the level descriptions are intended to indicate pitch and are not statutory. At levels 4 and 5, similar examples may be drawn from either the key stage 2 or the key stage 3 programmes of study.

The level descriptions provide the basis for making judgements about pupils' performance at the end of key stages 1, 2 and 3. At key stage 4, national qualifications are the main means of assessing attainment in science.

Range of levels within which the great majority of pupils are expected to work		Expected attainment for the majority of pupils at the end of the key stage	
Key stage 1	**1–3**	at age 7	**2**
Key stage 2	**2–5**	at age 11	**4**
Key stage 3	**3–7**	at age 14	**5/6**

Assessing attainment at the end of a key stage

In deciding on a pupil's level of attainment at the end of a key stage, teachers should judge which description best fits the pupil's performance. When doing so, each description should be considered alongside descriptions for adjacent levels.

Arrangements for statutory assessment at the end of each key stage are set out in detail in QCA's annual booklets about assessment and reporting arrangements.

---

[2] As defined by the Education Act 1996, section 353a.

Learning across the National Curriculum

The importance of science to pupils' education is set out on page 15. The handbooks for primary and secondary teachers also set out in general terms how the National Curriculum can promote learning across the curriculum in a number of areas such as spiritual, moral, social and cultural development, key skills and thinking skills. The examples below indicate specific ways in which the teaching of science can contribute to learning across the curriculum.

Promoting pupils' spiritual, moral, social and cultural development through science

For example, science provides opportunities to promote:

- *spiritual development,* through pupils sensing the natural, material, physical world they live in, reflecting on their part in it, and exploring questions such as when does life start and where does life come from?
- *moral development,* through helping pupils see the need to draw conclusions using observation and evidence rather than preconception or prejudice, and through discussion of the implications of the uses of scientific knowledge, including the recognition that such uses can have both beneficial and harmful effects
- *social development,* through helping pupils recognise how the formation of opinion and the justification of decisions can be informed by experimental evidence, and drawing attention to how different interpretations of scientific evidence can be used in discussing social issues
- *cultural development,* through helping pupils recognise how scientific discoveries and ideas have affected the way people think, feel, create, behave and live, and drawing attention to how cultural differences can influence the extent to which scientific ideas are accepted, used and valued.

Promoting key skills through science

For example, science provides opportunities for pupils to develop the key skills of:

- *communication,* through finding out about and communicating facts, ideas and opinions in a variety of contexts
- *application of number,* through collecting, considering and analysing first-hand and secondary data
- *IT,* through using a wide range of ICT
- *working with others,* through carrying out scientific investigations
- *improving own learning and performance,* through reflecting on what they have done and evaluating what they have achieved
- *problem solving,* through finding ways to answer scientific questions with creative solutions.

Promoting other aspects of the curriculum

For example, science provides opportunities to promote:
- *thinking skills*, through pupils engaging in the processes of scientific enquiry
- *enterprise and entrepreneurial skills*, through pupils learning about the work of scientists and of the ways in which scientific ideas are used in technological products and processes
- *work-related learning*, through studies of science-based industrial and commercial enterprises and through contacts with local scientists, engineers and workplaces
- *education for sustainable development*, through developing pupils' skills in decision making on the basis of sound science, the exploration of values and ethics relating to the applications of science and technology, and developing pupils' knowledge and understanding of some key concepts, such as diversity and interdependence.

The programmes of study for science

A common structure and design for all subjects

The programmes of study

The National Curriculum programmes of study have been given a common structure and a common design.

In each subject, at each key stage, the main column **1** contains the programme of study, which sets out two sorts of requirements:

- **Knowledge, skills and understanding** **2** – what has to be taught in the subject during the key stage
- **Breadth of study** – the contexts, activities, areas of study and range of experiences through which the **Knowledge, skills and understanding** should be taught.

Schools are not required by law to teach the content in grey type. This includes the examples in the main column **3** [printed inside square brackets], all text in the margins **4** and information and examples in the inclusion statement.

The programmes of study for English, mathematics and science

The programmes of study for English and science contain sections that correspond directly to the attainment targets for each subject. In mathematics this one-to-one correspondence does not hold for all key stages – see the mathematics programme of study for more information. In English, the three sections of the programme of study each contain **Breadth of study** requirements. In mathematics and science there is a single, separate set of **Breadth of study** requirements for each key stage.

The programmes of study in the non-core foundation subjects

In these subjects (except for citizenship) the programme of study simply contains two sets of requirements – **Knowledge, skills and understanding** and **Breadth of study**. The programmes of study for citizenship contain no **Breadth of study** requirements.

Information in the margins

At the start of each key stage, the margin begins with a summary **5** of the main things that pupils will learn during the key stage. The margins also contain four other types of non-statutory information:

- notes giving key information that should be taken into account when teaching the subject
- notes giving definitions of words and phrases in the programmes of study
- suggested opportunities for pupils to use information and communication technology (ICT) as they learn the subject
- some key links with other subjects indicating connections between teaching requirements, and suggesting how a requirement in one subject can build on the requirements in another in the same key stage.

Common structure and design

The referencing system
References work as follows:

A reference in ...	... reads ...	... and means ...
Physical education key stage 2	11a, 11b → links to other subjects These requirements build on Gg/2c.	Physical education key stage 2, requirements 11a and 11b build on geography (key stage 2), paragraph 2, requirement c.
Art and design key stage 1	4a → links to other subjects This requirement builds on Ma3/2a, 2c, 2d.	Art and design key stage 1, requirement 4a builds on mathematics (key stage 1), Ma3 Shape, space and measures, paragraph 2, requirements a, c and d.
Citizenship key stage 3	1a → links to other subjects This requirement builds on Hi/10, 13.	Citizenship key stage 3, requirement 1a builds on history (key stage 3) paragraphs 10 and 13.

The attainment targets
The attainment targets **6** are at the end of this booklet. They can be read alongside the programmes of study by folding out the flaps.

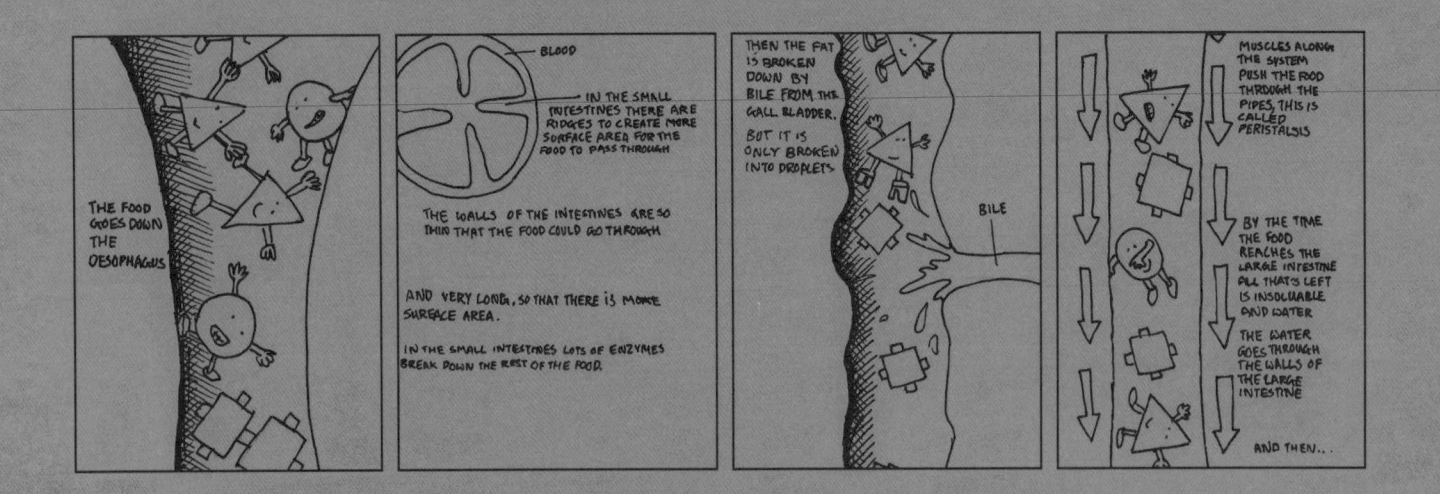

Science does not tell us everything that we want to know about life, or all we need to know. But it does provide us with the most robust information about the way the universe works that has so far become available to us.

Colin Tudge, Science Writer

Science is valuable because it meshes with all our lives and allows us to channel and use our spontaneous curiosity.

Professor Susan Greenfield, Director, Royal Institution

Studying science teaches us to be good at analysis and helps us to make complex things simple. It trains minds in a way that industry prizes.

Brendan O'Neill, Chief Executive, Imperial Chemical Industries PLC

Science is an integral part of modern culture. It stretches the imagination and creativity of young people. Its challenges are quite enormous.

Professor Malcolm Longair, Institute of Physics Fellow in Public Understanding of Physics, Head of Cavendish Laboratory, University of Cambridge

Forces

A force is a push or a pull.

Gravity

Gravity is a force which pulls you to the centre of the Earth.

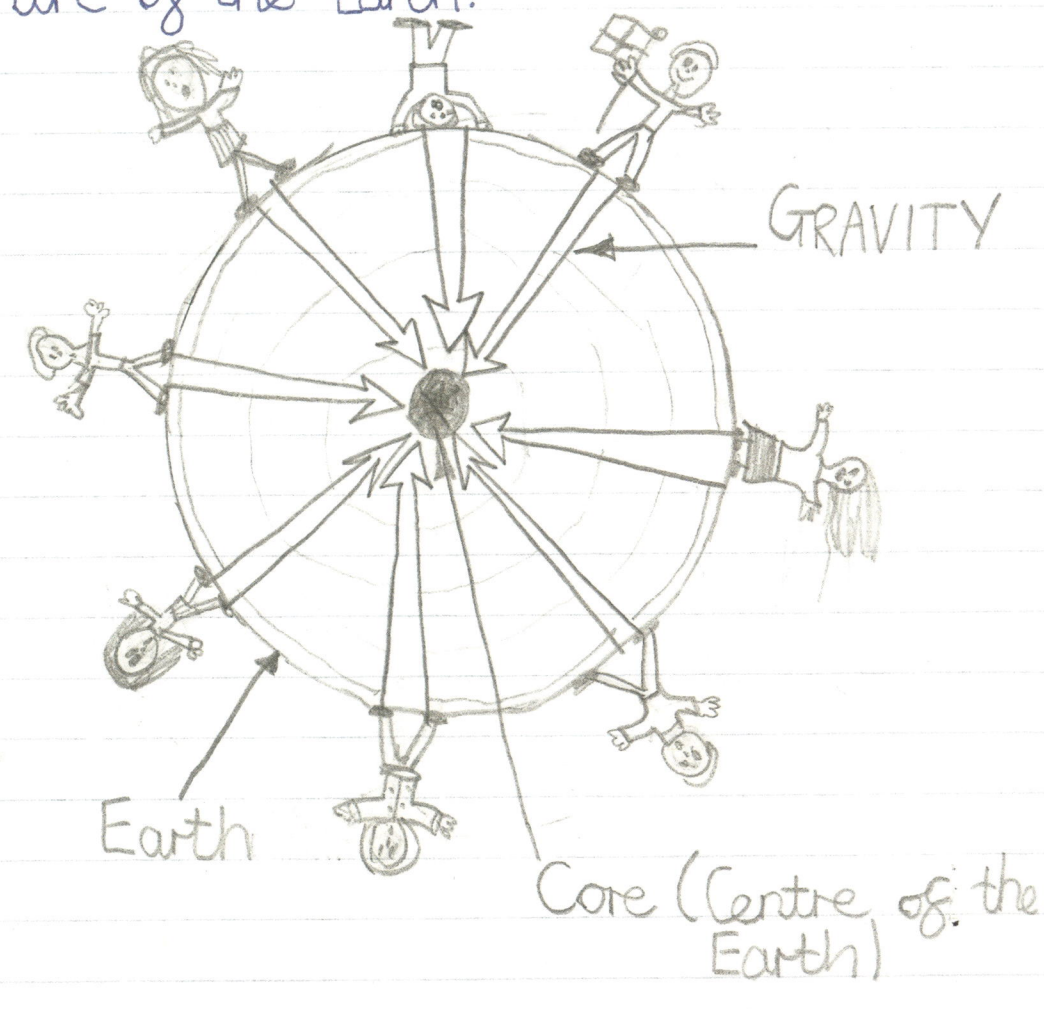

[Diagram showing figures standing around a circle (Earth) with arrows pointing inward to the centre, labelled "GRAVITY", "Earth", and "Core (Centre of the Earth)"]

The importance of science
Science stimulates and excites pupils' curiosity about phenomena and events in the world around them. It also satisfies this curiosity with knowledge. Because science links direct practical experience with ideas, it can engage learners at many levels. Scientific method is about developing and evaluating explanations through experimental evidence and modelling. This is a spur to critical and creative thought. Through science, pupils understand how major scientific ideas contribute to technological change – impacting on industry, business and medicine and improving quality of life. Pupils recognise the cultural significance of science and trace its worldwide development. They learn to question and discuss science-based issues that may affect their own lives, the direction of society and the future of the world.

Science key stage 1

Sc1 Scientific enquiry

Programme of study: science

Key stage 1

During key stage 1 pupils observe, explore and ask questions about living things, materials and phenomena. They begin to work together to collect evidence to help them answer questions and to link this to simple scientific ideas. They evaluate evidence and consider whether tests or comparisons are fair. They use reference materials to find out more about scientific ideas. They share their ideas and communicate them using scientific language, drawings, charts and tables.

Note
The general teaching requirement for health and safety applies in this subject.

2 → links to other subjects
These requirements build on En1/10.

2b → links to other subjects
This requirement builds on En2/7a, 7b.

2f → links to other subjects
This requirement builds on Ma3/4a, 4c.

Note for 2f
In the international system of units, kilogram (kg) is the unit of mass. In practice, mass is measured by weighing; scales measure or compare a force (a push or a pull). At key stage 1 it is acceptable to treat weight as synonymous with mass. At key stage 2 pupils will learn that the unit of weight (a type of force) is the newton.

In science, the term volume is preferred to capacity. The preferred unit is cubic centimetres, but at key stage 1 the unit litre (= 1000 cubic centimetres) is acceptable.

2g → links to other subjects
This requirement builds on Ma2/5a, 5b and ICT/3.

2i, 2j → links to other subjects
These requirements build on En1/1c, 3c and En3/1d, 1e.

Knowledge, skills and understanding

Teaching should ensure that **scientific enquiry** is taught through contexts taken from the sections on **life processes and living things**, **materials and their properties** and **physical processes**.

Sc1 Scientific enquiry

Ideas and evidence in science

1   Pupils should be taught that it is important to collect evidence by making observations and measurements when trying to answer a question.

Investigative skills

2   Pupils should be taught to:

   Planning

   a   ask questions [for example, 'How?', 'Why?', 'What will happen if … ?'] and decide how they might find answers to them

   b   use first-hand experience and simple information sources to answer questions

   c   think about what might happen before deciding what to do

   d   recognise when a test or comparison is unfair

   Obtaining and presenting evidence

   e   follow simple instructions to control the risks to themselves and to others

   f   explore, using the senses of sight, hearing, smell, touch and taste as appropriate, and make and record observations and measurements

   g   communicate what happened in a variety of ways, including using ICT [for example, in speech and writing, by drawings, tables, block graphs and pictograms]

   Considering evidence and evaluating

   h   make simple comparisons [for example, hand span, shoe size] and identify simple patterns or associations

   i   compare what happened with what they expected would happen, and try to explain it, drawing on their knowledge and understanding

   j   review their work and explain what they did to others.

Sc2 Life processes and living things

Life processes
1 Pupils should be taught:
   a the differences between things that are living and things that have never been alive
   b that animals, including humans, move, feed, grow, use their senses and reproduce
   c to relate life processes to animals and plants found in the local environment.

Humans and other animals
2 Pupils should be taught:
   a to recognise and compare the main external parts of the bodies of humans and other animals
   b that humans and other animals need food and water to stay alive
   c that taking exercise and eating the right types and amounts of food help humans to keep healthy
   d about the role of drugs as medicines
   e how to treat animals with care and sensitivity
   f that humans and other animals can produce offspring and that these offspring grow into adults
   g about the senses that enable humans and other animals to be aware of the world around them.

Green plants
3 Pupils should be taught:
   a to recognise that plants need light and water to grow
   b to recognise and name the leaf, flower, stem and root of flowering plants
   c that seeds grow into flowering plants.

Variation and classification
4 Pupils should be taught to:
   a recognise similarities and differences between themselves and others, and to treat others with sensitivity
   b group living things according to observable similarities and differences.

Living things in their environment
5 Pupils should be taught to:
   a find out about the different kinds of plants and animals in the local environment
   b identify similarities and differences between local environments and ways in which these affect animals and plants that are found there
   c care for the environment.

Science key stage 1

Sc2 Life processes and living things

2a → ICT opportunity
Pupils could use multimedia sources to make comparisons.

4 → ICT opportunity
Pupils could use data collected to compile a class database.

Science key stage 1

Sc3 Materials and their properties

1b → ICT opportunity
Pupils could use a software package to combine words and pictures about materials and objects.

Sc3 Materials and their properties

Grouping materials
1 Pupils should be taught to:
   a use their senses to explore and recognise the similarities and differences between materials
   b sort objects into groups on the basis of simple material properties [for example, roughness, hardness, shininess, ability to float, transparency and whether they are magnetic or non-magnetic]
   c recognise and name common types of material [for example, metal, plastic, wood, paper, rock] and recognise that some of them are found naturally
   d find out about the uses of a variety of materials [for example, glass, wood, wool] and how these are chosen for specific uses on the basis of their simple properties.

Changing materials
2 Pupils should be taught to:
   a find out how the shapes of objects made from some materials can be changed by some processes, including squashing, bending, twisting and stretching
   b explore and describe the way some everyday materials [for example, water, chocolate, bread, clay] change when they are heated or cooled.

Science key stage 1

Sc4 Physical processes

Sc4 Physical processes

Electricity

1   Pupils should be taught:
    a   about everyday appliances that use electricity
    b   about simple series circuits involving batteries, wires, bulbs and other components [for example, buzzers, motors]
    c   how a switch can be used to break a circuit.

Forces and motion

2   Pupils should be taught:
    a   to find out about, and describe the movement of, familiar things [for example, cars going faster, slowing down, changing direction]
    b   that both pushes and pulls are examples of forces
    c   to recognise that when things speed up, slow down or change direction, there is a cause [for example, a push or a pull].

Light and sound

3   Pupils should be taught:

    #### Light and dark
    a   to identify different light sources, including the Sun
    b   that darkness is the absence of light

    #### Making and detecting sounds
    c   that there are many kinds of sound and sources of sound
    d   that sounds travel away from sources, getting fainter as they do so, and that they are heard when they enter the ear.

2a → **links to other subjects**
This requirement builds on Ma3/3a, 3b.

3c → **ICT opportunity**
Pupils could use sensors to detect and compare sounds.

Science key stage 1

Breadth of study

2a → links to other subjects
This requirement builds on En1/1b, 8c, 10c and En3/9a, 9d.

Breadth of study

1   During the key stage, pupils should be taught the **Knowledge, skills and understanding** through:
    a   a range of domestic and environmental contexts that are familiar and of interest to them
    b   looking at the part science has played in the development of many useful things
    c   using a range of sources of information and data, including ICT-based sources
    d   using first-hand and secondary data to carry out a range of scientific investigations, including complete investigations.

2   During the key stage, pupils should be taught to:

    ## Communication
    a   use simple scientific language to communicate ideas and to name and describe living things, materials, phenomena and processes

    ## Health and safety
    b   recognise that there are hazards in living things, materials and physical processes, and assess risks and take action to reduce risks to themselves and others.

Programme of study: science

Key stage 2

Knowledge, skills and understanding

Teaching should ensure that **scientific enquiry** is taught through contexts taken from the sections on **life processes and living things**, **materials and their properties** and **physical processes**.

Sc1 Scientific enquiry

Ideas and evidence in science

1 Pupils should be taught:

   a that science is about thinking creatively to try to explain how living and non-living things work, and to establish links between causes and effects [for example, Jenner's vaccination work]

   b that it is important to test ideas using evidence from observation and measurement.

Investigative skills

2 Pupils should be taught to:

   Planning

   a ask questions that can be investigated scientifically and decide how to find answers

   b consider what sources of information, including first-hand experience and a range of other sources, they will use to answer questions

   c think about what might happen or try things out when deciding what to do, what kind of evidence to collect, and what equipment and materials to use

   d make a fair test or comparison by changing one factor and observing or measuring the effect while keeping other factors the same

   Obtaining and presenting evidence

   e use simple equipment and materials appropriately and take action to control risks

   f make systematic observations and measurements, including the use of ICT for datalogging

   g check observations and measurements by repeating them where appropriate

   h use a wide range of methods, including diagrams, drawings, tables, bar charts, line graphs and ICT, to communicate data in an appropriate and systematic manner

---

Science key stage 2

Sc1 Scientific enquiry

During key stage 2 pupils learn about a wider range of living things, materials and phenomena. They begin to make links between ideas and to explain things using simple models and theories. They apply their knowledge and understanding of scientific ideas to familiar phenomena, everyday things and their personal health. They begin to think about the positive and negative effects of scientific and technological developments on the environment and in other contexts. They carry out more systematic investigations, working on their own and with others. They use a range of reference sources in their work. They talk about their work and its significance, and communicate ideas using a wide range of scientific language, conventional diagrams, charts and graphs.

Note
The general teaching requirement for health and safety applies in this subject.

2 → links to other subjects
These requirements build on En1/10.

2b → links to other subjects
This requirement builds on En2/3.

2c, 2e, 2f → links to other subjects
These requirements build on Ma3/4a, 4b.

Note for 2c, 2e, 2f
In the international system of units, kilogram (kg) is the unit of mass. In practice mass is measured by weighing; scales measure or compare a force (a push or a pull). At key stage 2 pupils learn that the unit of weight (a type of force) is the newton.

In science the term volume is preferred to capacity. The preferred unit is cubic centimetres.

2f → links to other subjects
This requirement builds on ICT/2b.

2h → links to other subjects
This requirement builds on ICT/3.

Science key stage 2

Sc1 Scientific enquiry

2i, 2j → links to other subjects
These requirements build on Ma2/2i, 4a, 4d.

2i–2k → links to other subjects
These requirements build on Ma4/2.

Considering evidence and evaluating

i   make comparisons and identify simple patterns or associations in their own observations and measurements or other data
j   use observations, measurements or other data to draw conclusions
k   decide whether these conclusions agree with any prediction made and/or whether they enable further predictions to be made
l   use their scientific knowledge and understanding to explain observations, measurements or other data or conclusions
m   review their work and the work of others and describe its significance and limitations.

Science key stage 2
Sc2 Life processes and living things

Sc2 Life processes and living things

Life processes
1 Pupils should be taught:
   a that the life processes common to humans and other animals include nutrition, movement, growth and reproduction
   b that the life processes common to plants include growth, nutrition and reproduction
   c to make links between life processes in familiar animals and plants and the environments in which they are found.

Humans and other animals
2 Pupils should be taught:

   #### Nutrition
   a about the functions and care of teeth
   b about the need for food for activity and growth, and about the importance of an adequate and varied diet for health

   #### Circulation
   c that the heart acts as a pump to circulate the blood through vessels around the body, including through the lungs
   d about the effect of exercise and rest on pulse rate

   #### Movement
   e that humans and some other animals have skeletons and muscles to support and protect their bodies and to help them to move

   #### Growth and reproduction
   f about the main stages of the human life cycle

   #### Health
   g about the effects on the human body of tobacco, alcohol and other drugs, and how these relate to their personal health
   h about the importance of exercise for good health.

Green plants
3 Pupils should be taught:

   #### Growth and nutrition
   a the effect of light, air, water and temperature on plant growth
   b the role of the leaf in producing new material for growth
   c that the root anchors the plant, and that water and minerals are taken in through the root and transported through the stem to other parts of the plant

---

2b → ICT opportunity
Pupils could use a database or spreadsheet to analyse data about types of food in school lunches.

Note for 2c
Details of structure do not need to be taught.

2c, 2e, 2f → ICT opportunity
Pupils could use video or CD-ROM to see things that cannot be directly observed.

Science key stage 2

Sc2 Life processes and living things

4a → ICT opportunity
Pupils could use a branching database to develop and use keys.

5b → ICT opportunity
Pupils could use video or CD-ROM to compare non-local habitats.

5f → ICT opportunity
Pupils could use simulation software to show changes in the populations of micro-organisms in different conditions.

Reproduction

d   about the parts of the flower [for example, stigma, stamen, petal, sepal] and their role in the life cycle of flowering plants, including pollination, seed formation, seed dispersal and germination.

Variation and classification

4   Pupils should be taught:
   a   to make and use keys
   b   how locally occurring animals and plants can be identified and assigned to groups
   c   that the variety of plants and animals makes it important to identify them and assign them to groups.

Living things in their environment

5   Pupils should be taught:
   a   about ways in which living things and the environment need protection

Adaptation

   b   about the different plants and animals found in different habitats
   c   how animals and plants in two different habitats are suited to their environment

Feeding relationships

   d   to use food chains to show feeding relationships in a habitat
   e   about how nearly all food chains start with a green plant

Micro-organisms

   f   that micro-organisms are living organisms that are often too small to be seen, and that they may be beneficial [for example, in the breakdown of waste, in making bread] or harmful [for example, in causing disease, in causing food to go mouldy].

Science key stage 2
Sc3 Materials and their properties

Sc3 Materials and their properties

Grouping and classifying materials

1   Pupils should be taught:
   a   to compare everyday materials and objects on the basis of their material properties, including hardness, strength, flexibility and magnetic behaviour, and to relate these properties to everyday uses of the materials
   b   that some materials are better thermal insulators than others
   c   that some materials are better electrical conductors than others
   d   to describe and group rocks and soils on the basis of their characteristics, including appearance, texture and permeability
   e   to recognise differences between solids, liquids and gases, in terms of ease of flow and maintenance of shape and volume.

Changing materials

2   Pupils should be taught:
   a   to describe changes that occur when materials are mixed [for example, adding salt to water]
   b   to describe changes that occur when materials [for example, water, clay, dough] are heated or cooled
   c   that temperature is a measure of how hot or cold things are
   d   about reversible changes, including dissolving, melting, boiling, condensing, freezing and evaporating
   e   the part played by evaporation and condensation in the water cycle
   f   that non-reversible changes [for example, vinegar reacting with bicarbonate of soda, plaster of Paris with water] result in the formation of new materials that may be useful
   g   that burning materials [for example, wood, wax, natural gas] results in the formation of new materials and that this change is not usually reversible.

Separating mixtures of materials

3   Pupils should be taught:
   a   how to separate solid particles of different sizes by sieving [for example, those in soil]
   b   that some solids [for example, salt, sugar] dissolve in water to give solutions but some [for example, sand, chalk] do not
   c   how to separate insoluble solids from liquids by filtering
   d   how to recover dissolved solids by evaporating the liquid from the solution
   e   to use knowledge of solids, liquids and gases to decide how mixtures might be separated.

Note for 1e
Particle theory does not need to be taught.

2b → ICT opportunity
Pupils could use sensors to record temperature changes.

2e → ICT opportunity
Pupils could use CD-ROM or the internet to research water supplies in a range of localities.

Science key stage 2
Sc4 Physical processes

1a → ICT opportunity
Pupils could use simulation software to extend an investigation of components in a series circuit.

Note for 1b
Resistance does not need to be taught.

Note for 2b
Distinction between mass and weight need not be taught.

3f → ICT opportunity
Pupils could use sensors to detect and compare sounds made under different conditions.

Sc4 Physical processes

Electricity

1 Pupils should be taught:

Simple circuits

a   to construct circuits, incorporating a battery or power supply and a range of switches, to make electrical devices work [for example, buzzers, motors]

b   how changing the number or type of components [for example, batteries, bulbs, wires] in a series circuit can make bulbs brighter or dimmer

c   how to represent series circuits by drawings and conventional symbols, and how to construct series circuits on the basis of drawings and diagrams using conventional symbols.

Forces and motion

2 Pupils should be taught:

Types of force

a   about the forces of attraction and repulsion between magnets, and about the forces of attraction between magnets and magnetic materials

b   that objects are pulled downwards because of the gravitational attraction between them and the Earth

c   about friction, including air resistance, as a force that slows moving objects and may prevent objects from starting to move

d   that when objects [for example, a spring, a table] are pushed or pulled, an opposing pull or push can be felt

e   how to measure forces and identify the direction in which they act.

Light and sound

3 Pupils should be taught:

Everyday effects of light

a   that light travels from a source

b   that light cannot pass through some materials, and how this leads to the formation of shadows

c   that light is reflected from surfaces [for example, mirrors, polished metals]

Seeing

d   that we see things only when light from them enters our eyes

Vibration and sound

e   that sounds are made when objects [for example, strings on musical instruments] vibrate but that vibrations are not always directly visible

f   how to change the pitch and loudness of sounds produced by some vibrating objects [for example, a drum skin, a plucked string]

g   that vibrations from sound sources require a medium [for example, metal, wood, glass, air] through which to travel to the ear.

The Earth and beyond

4 Pupils should be taught:

The Sun, Earth and Moon

a that the Sun, Earth and Moon are approximately spherical

Periodic changes

b how the position of the Sun appears to change during the day, and how shadows change as this happens

c how day and night are related to the spin of the Earth on its own axis

d that the Earth orbits the Sun once each year, and that the Moon takes approximately 28 days to orbit the Earth.

Breadth of study

1 During the key stage, pupils should be taught the **Knowledge, skills and understanding** through:

a a range of domestic and environmental contexts that are familiar and of interest to them

b looking at the part science has played in the development of many useful things

c using a range of sources of information and data, including ICT-based sources

d using first-hand and secondary data to carry out a range of scientific investigations, including complete investigations.

2 During the key stage, pupils should be taught to:

Communication

a use appropriate scientific language and terms, including SI units of measurement [for example, metre, newton], to communicate ideas and explain the behaviour of living things, materials, phenomena and processes

Health and safety

b recognise that there are hazards in living things, materials and physical processes, and assess risks and take action to reduce risks to themselves and others.

4b–4d → **ICT opportunity**
Pupils could use video or CD-ROM to study models of the Sun, Earth and Moon system.

2a → **links to other subjects**
This requirement builds on En1/10a–10c and En3/9b–9d and Ma3/1a.

Science key stage 3

Sc1 Scientific enquiry

Programme of study: science

Key stage 3

During key stage 3 pupils build on their scientific knowledge and understanding and make connections between different areas of science. They use scientific ideas and models to explain phenomena and events, and to understand a range of familiar applications of science. They think about the positive and negative effects of scientific and technological developments on the environment and in other contexts. They take account of others' views and understand why opinions may differ. They do more quantitative work, carrying out investigations on their own and with others. They evaluate their work, in particular the strength of the evidence they and others have collected. They select and use a wide range of reference sources. They communicate clearly what they did and its significance. They learn how scientists work together on present-day scientific developments and about the importance of experimental evidence in supporting scientific ideas.

Note
The general teaching requirement for health and safety applies in this subject.

2 → links to other subjects
These requirements build on En1/10a.

2b → links to other subjects
This requirement builds on En2/4a–4c.

2d → ICT opportunity
Pupils could use data-handling software with fieldwork data.

2e → links to other subjects
This requirement builds on Ma4/1a, 2c.

2g → links to other subjects
This requirement builds on Ma3/4a and Ma4/3a, 3b and ICT/2b.

2i → links to other subjects
This requirement builds on Ma4/4a, 4b, 4h.

Knowledge, skills and understanding

Teaching should ensure that **scientific enquiry** is taught through contexts taken from the sections on **life processes and living things**, **materials and their properties** and **physical processes**.

Sc1 Scientific enquiry

Ideas and evidence in science

1   Pupils should be taught:

   a   about the interplay between empirical questions, evidence and scientific explanations using historical and contemporary examples [for example, Lavoisier's work on burning, the possible causes of global warming]

   b   that it is important to test explanations by using them to make predictions and by seeing if evidence matches the predictions

   c   about the ways in which scientists work today and how they worked in the past, including the roles of experimentation, evidence and creative thought in the development of scientific ideas.

Investigative skills

2   Pupils should be taught to:

   Planning

   a   use scientific knowledge and understanding to turn ideas into a form that can be investigated, and to decide on an appropriate approach

   b   decide whether to use evidence from first-hand experience or secondary sources

   c   carry out preliminary work and to make predictions, where appropriate

   d   consider key factors that need to be taken into account when collecting evidence, and how evidence may be collected in contexts [for example, fieldwork, surveys] in which the variables cannot readily be controlled

   e   decide the extent and range of data to be collected and the techniques, equipment and materials to use [for example, appropriate sample size for biological work]

   Obtaining and presenting evidence

   f   use a range of equipment and materials appropriately and take action to control risks to themselves and to others

   g   make observations and measurements, including the use of ICT for datalogging [for example, variables changing over time] to an appropriate degree of precision

   h   make sufficient relevant observations and measurements to reduce error and obtain reliable evidence

   i   use a wide range of methods, including diagrams, tables, charts, graphs and ICT, to represent and communicate qualitative and quantitative data

Science key stage 3
Sc1 Scientific enquiry

Considering evidence

j use diagrams, tables, charts and graphs, including lines of best fit, to identify and describe patterns or relationships in data

k use observations, measurements and other data to draw conclusions

l decide to what extent these conclusions support a prediction or enable further predictions to be made

m use their scientific knowledge and understanding to explain and interpret observations, measurements or other data, and conclusions

Evaluating

n consider anomalies in observations or measurements and try to explain them

o consider whether the evidence is sufficient to support any conclusions or interpretations made

p suggest improvements to the methods used, where appropriate.

2j–2o → links to other subjects
These requirements build on Ma4/5a–5g, 5j.

2j → ICT opportunity
Pupils could use data-handling software to create, analyse and evaluate charts and graphs.

Science key stage 3

Sc2 Life processes and living things

2a → ICT opportunity
Pupils could use databases or spreadsheets to record, analyse and evaluate information about diets.

Sc2 Life processes and living things

Cells and cell functions

1 Pupils should be taught:
  a that animal and plant cells can form tissues, and tissues can form organs
  b the functions of chloroplasts and cell walls in plant cells and the functions of the cell membrane, cytoplasm and nucleus in both plant and animal cells
  c ways in which some cells, including ciliated epithelial cells, sperm, ova, and root hair cells, are adapted to their functions
  d that fertilisation in humans and flowering plants is the fusion of a male and a female cell
  e to relate cells and cell functions to life processes in a variety of organisms.

Humans as organisms

2 Pupils should be taught:

  #### Nutrition
  a about the need for a balanced diet containing carbohydrates, proteins, fats, minerals, vitamins, fibre and water, and about foods that are sources of these
  b the principles of digestion, including the role of enzymes in breaking down large molecules into smaller ones
  c that the products of digestion are absorbed into the bloodstream and transported throughout the body, and that waste material is egested
  d that food is used as a fuel during respiration to maintain the body's activity and as a raw material for growth and repair

  #### Movement
  e the role of the skeleton and joints and the principle of antagonistic muscle pairs [for example, biceps and triceps] in movement

  #### Reproduction
  f about the physical and emotional changes that take place during adolescence
  g about the human reproductive system, including the menstrual cycle and fertilisation
  h how the fetus develops in the uterus, including the role of the placenta

  #### Breathing
  i the role of lung structure in gas exchange, including the effect of smoking

  #### Respiration
  j that aerobic respiration involves a reaction in cells between oxygen and food, in which glucose is broken down into carbon dioxide and water
  k to summarise aerobic respiration in a word equation
  l that the reactants and products of respiration are transported throughout the body in the bloodstream

Science key stage 3

Sc2 Life processes and living things

Health

m   that the abuse of alcohol, solvents, and other drugs affects health

n   how the growth and reproduction of bacteria and the replication of viruses can affect health, and how the body's natural defences may be enhanced by immunisation and medicines.

Green plants as organisms

3   Pupils should be taught:

Nutrition and growth

a   that plants need carbon dioxide, water and light for photosynthesis, and produce biomass and oxygen

b   to summarise photosynthesis in a word equation

c   that nitrogen and other elements, in addition to carbon, oxygen and hydrogen, are required for plant growth

d   the role of root hairs in absorbing water and minerals from the soil

Respiration

e   that plants carry out aerobic respiration.

Variation, classification and inheritance

4   Pupils should be taught:

Variation

a   about environmental and inherited causes of variation within a species

Classification

b   to classify living things into the major taxonomic groups

Inheritance

c   that selective breeding can lead to new varieties.

Living things in their environment

5   Pupils should be taught:

Adaptation and competition

a   about ways in which living things and the environment can be protected, and the importance of sustainable development

b   that habitats support a diversity of plants and animals that are interdependent

c   how some organisms are adapted to survive daily and seasonal changes in their habitats

d   how predation and competition for resources affect the size of populations [for example, bacteria, growth of vegetation]

Feeding relationships

e   about food webs composed of several food chains, and how food chains can be quantified using pyramids of numbers

f   how toxic materials can accumulate in food chains.

2n → ICT opportunity
Pupils could use simulation software to model changes in populations of bacteria in different conditions.

3a → ICT opportunity
Pupils could use sensors to record or use simulation software to model factors that affect photosynthesis.

5f → ICT opportunity
Pupils could use simulation software to explore toxic materials in food chains.

Science key stage 3
Sc3 Materials and their properties

1a → ICT opportunity
Pupils could search a database for information about properties of materials.

2a → ICT opportunity
Pupils could use dataloggers to collect, analyse and evaluate changes of temperature and mass.

Sc3 Materials and their properties

Classifying materials

1 Pupils should be taught:

   #### Solids, liquids and gases
   a how materials can be characterised by melting point, boiling point and density
   b how the particle theory of matter can be used to explain the properties of solids, liquids and gases, including changes of state, gas pressure and diffusion

   #### Elements, compounds and mixtures
   c that the elements are shown in the periodic table and consist of atoms, which can be represented by symbols
   d how elements vary widely in their physical properties, including appearance, state at room temperature, magnetic properties and thermal and electrical conductivity, and how these properties can be used to classify elements as metals or non-metals
   e how elements combine through chemical reactions to form compounds [for example, water, carbon dioxide, magnesium oxide, sodium chloride, most minerals] with a definite composition
   f to represent compounds by formulae and to summarise reactions by word equations
   g that mixtures [for example, air, sea water and most rocks] are composed of constituents that are not combined
   h how to separate mixtures into their constituents using distillation, chromatography and other appropriate methods.

Changing materials

2 Pupils should be taught:

   #### Physical changes
   a that when physical changes [for example, changes of state, formation of solutions] take place, mass is conserved
   b about the variation of solubility with temperature, the formation of saturated solutions, and the differences in solubility of solutes in different solvents
   c to relate changes of state to energy transfers

   #### Geological changes
   d how forces generated by expansion, contraction and the freezing of water can lead to the physical weathering of rocks
   e about the formation of rocks by processes that take place over different timescales, and that the mode of formation determines their texture and the minerals they contain

f how igneous rocks are formed by the cooling of magma, sedimentary rocks by processes including the deposition of rock fragments or organic material, or as a result of evaporation, and metamorphic rocks by the action of heat and pressure on existing rocks

Chemical reactions

g how mass is conserved when chemical reactions take place because the same atoms are present, although combined in different ways

h that virtually all materials, including those in living systems, are made through chemical reactions, and to recognise the importance of chemical change in everyday situations [for example, ripening fruit, setting superglue, cooking food]

i about possible effects of burning fossil fuels on the environment [for example, production of acid rain, carbon dioxide and solid particles] and how these effects can be minimised.

Patterns of behaviour

3 Pupils should be taught:

Metals

a how metals react with oxygen, water, acids and oxides of other metals, and what the products of these reactions are

b about the displacement reactions that take place between metals and solutions of salts of other metals

c how a reactivity series of metals can be determined by considering these reactions, and used to make predictions about other reactions

Acids and bases

d to use indicators to classify solutions as acidic, neutral or alkaline, and to use the pH scale as a measure of the acidity of a solution

e how metals and bases, including carbonates, react with acids, and what the products of these reactions are

f about some everyday applications of neutralisation [for example, the treatment of indigestion, the treatment of acid soil, the manufacture of fertilizer]

g how acids in the environment can lead to corrosion of some metals and chemical weathering of rock [for example, limestone]

h to identify patterns in chemical reactions.

2i → **ICT opportunity**
Pupils could use the internet to find up-to-date information about environmental issues.

3a → **ICT opportunity**
Pupils could use video or CD-ROM to see reactions that are dangerous.

Science key stage 3
Sc4 Physical processes

1a → ICT opportunity
Pupils could use simulation software to investigate and model circuits.

2a, 2f, 2g → links to other subjects
These requirements build on Ma2/5f.

Sc4 Physical processes

Electricity and magnetism
1 Pupils should be taught:

Circuits

a how to design and construct series and parallel circuits, and how to measure current and voltage

b that the current in a series circuit depends on the number of cells and the number and nature of other components and that current is not 'used up' by components

c that energy is transferred from batteries and other sources to other components in electrical circuits

Magnetic fields

d about magnetic fields as regions of space where magnetic materials experience forces, and that like magnetic poles repel and unlike poles attract

Electromagnets

e that a current in a coil produces a magnetic field pattern similar to that of a bar magnet

f how electromagnets are constructed and used in devices [for example, relays, lifting magnets].

Forces and motion
2 Pupils should be taught:

Force and linear motion

a how to determine the speed of a moving object and to use the quantitative relationship between speed, distance and time

b that the weight of an object on Earth is the result of the gravitational attraction between its mass and that of the Earth

c that unbalanced forces change the speed or direction of movement of objects and that balanced forces produce no change in the movement of an object

d ways in which frictional forces, including air resistance, affect motion [for example, streamlining cars, friction between tyre and road]

Force and rotation

e that forces can cause objects to turn about a pivot

f the principle of moments and its application to situations involving one pivot

Force and pressure

g the quantitative relationship between force, area and pressure and its application [for example, the use of skis and snowboards, the effect of sharp blades, hydraulic brakes].

Science key stage 3

Sc4 Physical processes

Light and sound

3   Pupils should be taught:

The behaviour of light

a   that light travels in a straight line at a finite speed in a uniform medium
b   that non-luminous objects are seen because light scattered from them enters the eye
c   how light is reflected at plane surfaces
d   how light is refracted at the boundary between two different materials
e   that white light can be dispersed to give a range of colours
f   the effect of colour filters on white light and how coloured objects appear in white light and in other colours of light

Hearing

g   that sound causes the eardrum to vibrate and that different people have different audible ranges
h   some effects of loud sounds on the ear [for example, temporary deafness]

Vibration and sound

i   that light can travel through a vacuum but sound cannot, and that light travels much faster than sound
j   the relationship between the loudness of a sound and the amplitude of the vibration causing it
k   the relationship between the pitch of a sound and the frequency of the vibration causing it.

The Earth and beyond

4   Pupils should be taught:

The solar system

a   how the movement of the Earth causes the apparent daily and annual movement of the Sun and other stars
b   the relative positions of the Earth, Sun and planets in the solar system
c   about the movements of planets around the Sun and to relate these to gravitational forces
d   that the Sun and other stars are light sources and that the planets and other bodies are seen by reflected light
e   about the use of artificial satellites and probes to observe the Earth and to explore the solar system.

Energy resources and energy transfer

5   Pupils should be taught:

Energy resources

a   about the variety of energy resources, including oil, gas, coal, biomass, food, wind, waves and batteries, and the distinction between renewable and non-renewable resources

---

4a, 4c, 4e → ICT opportunity
Pupils could use video or CD-ROM to study the solar system.

5a, 5c → ICT opportunity
Pupils could use the internet to find up-to-date information about energy resources.

Science key stage 3
Breadth of study

2a → **links to other subjects**
This requirement builds on En1/1e and En3/9b–9d and Ma2/1g.

    b about the Sun as the ultimate source of most of the Earth's energy resources and to relate this to how coal, oil and gas are formed

    c that electricity is generated by means of a variety of energy resources

Conservation of energy

    d the distinction between temperature and heat, and that differences in temperature can lead to transfer of energy

    e ways in which energy can be usefully transferred and stored

    f how energy is transferred by the movement of particles in conduction, convection and evaporation, and that energy is transferred directly by radiation

    g that although energy is always conserved, it may be dissipated, reducing its availability as a resource.

Breadth of study

1 During the key stage, pupils should be taught the **Knowledge, skills and understanding** through:
    a a range of domestic, industrial and environmental contexts
    b considering ways in which science is applied in technological developments
    c considering the benefits and drawbacks of scientific and technological developments, including those related to the environment, health and quality of life
    d using a range of sources of information, including ICT-based sources
    e using first-hand and secondary data to carry out a range of scientific investigations, including complete investigations
    f using quantitative approaches where appropriate, including calculations based on simple relationships between physical quantities.

2 During the key stage, pupils should be taught to:

Communication

    a use scientific language, conventions and symbols, including SI units, word equations and chemical symbols, formulae and equations, where appropriate, to communicate scientific ideas and to provide scientific explanations based on evidence

Health and safety

    b recognise that there are hazards in living things, materials and physical processes, and assess risks and take action to reduce risks to themselves and others.

Programme of study: single science

Key stage 4

Single science key stage 4

Sc1 Scientific enquiry

Knowledge, skills and understanding

Teaching should ensure that **scientific enquiry** is taught through contexts taken from the sections on **life processes and living things**, **materials and their properties** and **physical processes**.

Sc1 Scientific enquiry

Ideas and evidence in science

1 Pupils should be taught:
   a how scientific ideas are presented, evaluated and disseminated [for example, by publication, review by other scientists]
   b how scientific controversies can arise from different ways of interpreting empirical evidence [for example, Darwin's theory of evolution]
   c ways in which scientific work may be affected by the contexts in which it takes place [for example, social, historical, moral, spiritual], and how these contexts may affect whether or not ideas are accepted
   d to consider the power and limitations of science in addressing industrial, social and environmental questions, including the kinds of questions science can and cannot answer, uncertainties in scientific knowledge, and the ethical issues involved.

Investigative skills

2 Pupils should be taught to:

   Planning
   a use scientific knowledge and understanding to turn ideas into a form that can be investigated, and to plan an appropriate strategy
   b decide whether to use evidence from first-hand experience or secondary sources
   c carry out preliminary work and make predictions, where appropriate
   d consider key factors that need to be taken into account when collecting evidence, and how evidence can be collected in contexts [for example, fieldwork, surveys] in which the variables cannot readily be controlled
   e decide the extent and range of data to be collected [for example, appropriate sample size for biological work] and the techniques, equipment and materials to use

   Obtaining and presenting evidence
   f use a wide range of equipment and materials appropriately, and manage their working environment to ensure the safety of themselves and others
   g make observations and measurements, including the use of ICT for datalogging [for example, to monitor several variables at the same time] to a degree of precision appropriate to the context
   h make sufficient observations and measurements to reduce error and obtain reliable evidence

---

During key stage 4 pupils learn about a wider range of scientific ideas and consider them in greater depth, laying the foundations for further study. They explore how technological advances relate to the scientific ideas underpinning them. They consider the power and limitations of science in addressing industrial, ethical and environmental issues, and how different groups have different views about the role of science. When they carry out investigations they use a range of approaches and select appropriate reference sources, working on their own and with others. They do more quantitative work and evaluate critically the evidence collected and conclusions drawn. They communicate their ideas clearly and precisely in a variety of ways. They see how scientists work together to develop new ideas, how new theories may, at first, give rise to controversy and how social and cultural contexts may affect the extent to which theories are accepted.

Note
The general teaching requirement for health and safety applies in this subject.

1a → links to other subjects
This requirement builds on En2/1a, 1c, 1d.

2 → links to other subjects
These requirements build on En1/10a.

2d → ICT opportunity
Pupils could use data-handling software to analyse data from fieldwork.

2e → links to other subjects
This requirement builds on Ma4/2c–2e (foundation and higher).

2g, 2h → links to other subjects
These requirements build on Ma3/4a and Ma4/3a, 3b (foundation and higher).

2g → links to other subjects
This requirement builds on ICT/1.

37

Single science key stage 4

Sc1 Scientific enquiry

2j → links to other subjects
This requirement builds on Ma4/4a, 4b, 4h (foundation) and Ma4/4a, 4i (higher) and ICT/3.

2k → links to other subjects
This requirement builds on Ma4/5b, 5c (foundation and higher).

2l → links to other subjects
This requirement builds on Ma2/4c (foundation) and Ma2/4b (higher).

2m–2q → links to other subjects
These requirements build on Ma4/5a–5f, 5i (foundation and higher).

i judge the level of uncertainty in observations and measurements [for example, by using the variation in repeat measurements to judge the likely accuracy of the average measured value]

j represent and communicate qualitative and quantitative data using diagrams, tables, charts, graphs and ICT

Considering evidence

k use diagrams, tables, charts and graphs, and identify and explain patterns or relationships in data

l present the results of calculations to an appropriate degree of accuracy

m use observations, measurements or other data to draw conclusions

n explain to what extent these conclusions support any prediction made, and enable further predictions to be made

o use scientific knowledge and understanding to explain and interpret observations, measurements or other data, and conclusions

Evaluating

p consider anomalous data giving reasons for rejecting or accepting them, and consider the reliability of data in terms of the uncertainty of measurements and observations

q consider whether the evidence collected is sufficient to support any conclusions or interpretations made

r suggest improvements to the methods used

s suggest further investigations.

Sc2 Life processes and living things

Cell activity

1   Pupils should be taught:
    a   that the nucleus contains chromosomes that carry the genes
    b   how cells divide by mitosis during growth, and by meiosis to produce gametes
    c   to relate ways in which animals function as organisms to cell structure and activity.

Humans as organisms

2   Pupils should be taught:

    #### Nutrition
    a   the processes of digestion, including the function of organs and the role of enzymes, stomach acid and bile

    #### Circulation
    b   the composition and functions of blood

    #### Nervous system
    c   the pathway taken by impulses in response to a variety of stimuli
    d   how the reflex arc makes rapid response to a stimulus possible
    e   how the eye functions in response to light

    #### Hormones
    f   the way in which hormonal control occurs, including the effects of sex hormones
    g   some medical uses of hormones, including the control and promotion of fertility

    #### Homeostasis
    h   the importance of maintaining a constant internal environment
    i   how waste products of body functions are removed by the kidneys
    j   how the kidneys regulate the water content of the body
    k   how humans maintain a constant body temperature

    #### Health
    l   the defence mechanisms of the body, including the role of the skin and blood
    m   the effects of solvents, alcohol, tobacco and other drugs on body functions.

2d → ICT opportunity
Pupils could use multimedia simulation of nerve impulse.

Single science key stage 4

Sc2 Life processes and living things

3g → ICT opportunity
Pupils could use the internet to find out about current developments and issues.

4a → ICT opportunity
Pupils could use spreadsheets to model the effects of competition and predation.

Variation, inheritance and evolution

3 Pupils should be taught:

Variation

a how variation arises from genetic causes, environmental causes, and a combination of both

b that sexual reproduction is a source of genetic variation, while asexual reproduction produces clones

c that mutation is a source of genetic variation and has a number of causes

Inheritance

d how sex is determined in humans

e the mechanism of monohybrid inheritance where there are dominant and recessive alleles

f that some diseases are inherited

g the basic principles of cloning, selective breeding and genetic engineering

Evolution

h that the fossil record is evidence for evolution

i how variation and selection may lead to evolution or to extinction.

Living things in their environment

4 Pupils should be taught:

Adaptation and competition

a how the distribution and relative abundance of organisms in habitats can be explained using ideas of interdependence, adaptation, competition and predation

b how the impact of humans on the environment depends on social and economic factors, including population size, industrial processes and levels of consumption and waste

c about the importance of sustainable development.

Sc3 Materials and their properties

Classifying materials

1 Pupils should be taught:

   Atomic structure
   a that atoms consist of nuclei and electrons
   b about a model of the way electrons are arranged in atoms
   c how the reactions of elements depend on the arrangement of electrons in their atoms.

Changing materials

2 Pupils should be taught:

   Useful products from organic sources
   a how the mixture of substances in crude oil, most of which are hydrocarbons, can be separated by fractional distillation
   b the use of some of the products from crude oil distillation as fuels
   c the products of burning hydrocarbons
   d how addition polymers can be formed from the products of crude oil by cracking and polymerisation
   e some uses of addition polymers.

Patterns of behaviour

3 Pupils should be taught:

   The periodic table
   a that there are approximately 100 elements and that all materials are composed of one or more of these
   b that the periodic table shows all the elements, arranged in order of ascending atomic number
   c the connection between the arrangement of outer electrons and the position of an element in the periodic table
   d that elements in the same group of the periodic table have similar properties
   e how the properties of elements change gradually from the top to the bottom of a group, illustrated by the study of at least one group

   Chemical reactions
   f about different types of chemical reaction, including neutralisation, oxidation, reduction and thermal decomposition, and examples of how these are used to make new materials
   g to recognise patterns in chemical reactions

Single science key stage 4
Sc3 Materials and their properties

1b, 1c → ICT opportunity
Pupils could use software simulations to explore models of the atom and reactions.

2b, 2c, 2e → ICT opportunity
Pupils could use the internet to find out about products and processes.

3c–3e → ICT opportunity
Pupils could use a database of the elements to explore patterns.

Single science key stage 4
Sc3 Materials and their properties

3h, 3i → ICT opportunity
Pupils could use dataloggers to analyse and evaluate reaction data.

3i → links to other subjects
This requirement builds on Ma4/5c (foundation and higher).

Rates of reaction

h about the great variation in the rates at which different reactions take place
i how the rates of reactions can be altered by varying temperature or concentration, or by changing the surface area of a solid reactant, or by adding a catalyst
j how the rates of many reactions depend on the frequency and energy of collisions between particles

Reactions involving enzymes

k how enzymes may be used in biotechnology.

Sc4 Physical processes

Electricity

1 Pupils should be taught:

Circuits

a   that resistors are heated when a charge flows through them
b   the qualitative effect of changing resistance on the current in a circuit
c   the quantitative relationship between resistance, voltage and current
d   how current varies with voltage in a range of devices [for example, resistors, filament bulbs, diodes, light dependent resistors (LDRs) and thermistors]

Mains electricity

e   the difference between direct current (dc) and alternating current (ac)
f   the functions of the live, neutral and earth wires in the domestic mains supply, and the use of insulation, earthing, fuses and circuit breakers to protect users of electrical equipment
g   how electrical heating is used in a variety of ways in domestic contexts
h   how measurements of energy transferred are used to calculate the costs of using common domestic appliances.

Waves

2 Pupils should be taught:

Characteristics of waves

a   about the reflection and refraction of waves, including light and sound as examples of transverse and longitudinal waves
b   the meaning of frequency, wavelength and amplitude of a wave

The electromagnetic spectrum

c   that the electromagnetic spectrum includes radio waves, microwaves, infrared, visible light, ultraviolet waves, X-rays and gamma rays
d   some ways in which microwaves, infrared and ultraviolet waves are used and the potential dangers of these
e   some uses of X-rays and gamma rays in medicine
f   that radio waves, microwaves, infrared and visible light carry information over large and small distances, including global transmission via satellites
g   the difference between analogue and digital signals

Sound and ultrasound

h   about sound and ultrasound waves, and some medical and other uses of ultrasound.

1c → links to other subjects
This requirement builds on Ma2/5f (foundation) and Ma2/5g (higher).

1d → links to other subjects
This requirement builds on Ma4/5c (foundation and higher).

1c, 1d → ICT opportunity
Pupils could use dataloggers to investigate relationships.

2a, 2b → ICT opportunity
Pupils could use CD-ROM software to explore wave models.

Single science key stage 4
Sc4 Physical processes

Single science key stage 4

Sc4 Physical processes

3a, 3b → ICT opportunity
Pupils could use video or CD-ROM software to simulate movements in the solar system and universe.

4b → ICT opportunity
Pupils could use a spreadsheet to model energy loss in a house.

The Earth and beyond

3   Pupils should be taught:

   #### The solar system and the wider universe
   a   the relative positions and sizes of planets, stars and other bodies in the universe [for example, comets, meteors, galaxies, black holes]
   b   how gravity acts as a force throughout the universe
   c   how stars evolve over a long timescale
   d   about some ideas used to explain the origin and evolution of the universe
   e   about the search for evidence of life elsewhere in the universe.

Energy resources and energy transfer

4   Pupils should be taught:

   #### Energy transfer
   a   how insulation is used to reduce transfer of energy from hotter to colder objects
   b   about the efficient use of energy, the need for economical use of energy resources, and the environmental implications of generating energy

   #### Electromagnetic effects
   c   how simple ac generators work
   d   how energy is transferred from power stations to consumers.

Radioactivity

5   Pupils should be taught:
   a   that radioactivity arises from the breakdown of an unstable nucleus
   b   about some sources of the ionising radiation found in all environments
   c   the characteristics of alpha and beta particles and of gamma radiation
   d   the beneficial and harmful effects of radiation on matter and living organisms.

Single science key stage 4
Breadth of study

Breadth of study

1 During the key stage, pupils should be taught the **Knowledge, skills and understanding** through:
   a a range of domestic, industrial and environmental contexts
   b considering ways in which science is applied in technological developments
   c considering and evaluating the benefits and drawbacks of scientific and technological developments, including those related to the environment, personal health and quality of life, and those raising ethical issues
   d using a range of sources of information, including ICT-based sources
   e using first-hand and secondary data to carry out a range of scientific investigations, including complete investigations
   f using quantitative approaches, where appropriate, including calculations based on relationships between physical quantities.

2 During the key stage, pupils should be taught to:

   ### Communication
   a use a wide range of scientific, technical and mathematical language, symbols and conventions, including SI units, balanced chemical equations and standard form to communicate ideas and develop an argument

   ### Health and safety
   b recognise that there are hazards in living things, materials and physical processes, and assess risks and take action to reduce risks to themselves and others.

2a → **links to other subjects**
This requirement builds on En1/1e and En3/9b–9d and Ma2/1f (foundation) and Ma2/1h (higher).

Double science key stage 4

Sc1 Scientific enquiry

Programme of study: double science

Key stage 4

Knowledge, skills and understanding

Teaching should ensure that **scientific enquiry** is taught through contexts taken from the sections on **life processes and living things**, **materials and their properties** and **physical processes**.

Sc1 Scientific enquiry

Ideas and evidence in science

1 Pupils should be taught:
   a how scientific ideas are presented, evaluated and disseminated [for example, by publication, review by other scientists]
   b how scientific controversies can arise from different ways of interpreting empirical evidence [for example, Darwin's theory of evolution]
   c ways in which scientific work may be affected by the contexts in which it takes place [for example, social, historical, moral and spiritual], and how these contexts may affect whether or not ideas are accepted
   d to consider the power and limitations of science in addressing industrial, social and environmental questions, including the kinds of questions science can and cannot answer, uncertainties in scientific knowledge, and the ethical issues involved.

Investigative skills

2 Pupils should be taught to:

   Planning
   a use scientific knowledge and understanding to turn ideas into a form that can be investigated, and to plan an appropriate strategy
   b decide whether to use evidence from first-hand experience or secondary sources
   c carry out preliminary work and make predictions, where appropriate
   d consider key factors that need to be taken into account when collecting evidence, and how evidence can be collected in contexts [for example, fieldwork, surveys] in which the variables cannot readily be controlled
   e decide the extent and range of data to be collected [for example, appropriate sample size for biological work], and the techniques, equipment and materials to use

   Obtaining and presenting evidence
   f use a wide range of equipment and materials appropriately, and manage their working environment to ensure the safety of themselves and others
   g make observations and measurements, including the use of ICT for datalogging [for example, to monitor several variables at the same time] to a degree of precision appropriate to the context
   h make sufficient observations and measurements to reduce error and obtain reliable evidence

---

During key stage 4 pupils learn about a wider range of scientific ideas and consider them in greater depth, laying the foundations for further study. They explore how technological advances relate to the scientific ideas underpinning them. They consider the power and limitations of science in addressing industrial, ethical and environmental issues, and how different groups have different views about the role of science. When they carry out investigations they use a range of approaches and select appropriate reference sources, working on their own and with others. They do more quantitative work and evaluate critically the evidence collected and conclusions drawn. They communicate their ideas clearly and precisely in a variety of ways. They see how scientists work together to develop new ideas, how new theories may, at first, give rise to controversy and how social and cultural contexts may affect the extent to which theories are accepted.

Note
The general teaching requirement for health and safety applies in this subject.

1a → links to other subjects
This requirement builds on En2/1a, 1c, 1d.

2 → links to other subjects
These requirements build on En1/10a.

2d → ICT opportunity
Pupils could use data-handling software to analyse data from fieldwork.

2e → links to other subjects
This requirement builds on Ma4/2c–2e (foundation and higher).

2g, 2h → links to other subjects
These requirements build on Ma3/4a and Ma4/3a, 3b (foundation and higher).

2g → links to other subjects
This requirement builds on ICT/1.

Double science key stage 4

Sc1 Scientific enquiry

i judge the level of uncertainty in observations and measurements [for example, by using the variation in repeat measurements to judge the likely accuracy of the average measured value]

j represent and communicate qualitative and quantitative data using diagrams, tables, charts, graphs and ICT

Considering evidence

k use diagrams, tables, charts and graphs, and identify and explain patterns or relationships in data

l present the results of calculations to an appropriate degree of accuracy

m use observations, measurements or other data to draw conclusions

n explain to what extent these conclusions support any predictions made, and enable further predictions to be made

o use scientific knowledge and understanding to explain and interpret observations, measurements or other data, and conclusions

Evaluating

p consider anomalous data giving reasons for rejecting or accepting them, and consider the reliability of data in terms of the uncertainty of measurements and observations

q consider whether the evidence collected is sufficient to support any conclusions or interpretations made

r suggest improvements to the methods used

s suggest further investigations.

2j → links to other subjects
This requirement builds on Ma4/4a, 4b, 4h (foundation) and Ma4/4a, 4i (higher) and ICT/3.

2k → links to other subjects
This requirement builds on Ma4/5b, 5c (foundation and higher).

2k → ICT opportunity
Pupils could use data-handling software to create, analyse and evaluate charts and graphs of data.

2l → links to other subjects
This requirement builds on Ma2/4c (foundation) and Ma2/4b (higher).

2m–2q → links to other subjects
These requirements build on Ma4/5a–5f, 5i (foundation and higher).

Double science key stage 4
Sc2 Life processes and living things

2d, 2h → ICT opportunity
Pupils could use multimedia sources to see things that cannot readily be observed.

Sc2 Life processes and living things

Cell activity

1 Pupils should be taught:
   a about similarities and differences in structure between plant and animal cells
   b how substances enter and leave cells through the cell membrane by diffusion, osmosis and active transport
   c that the nucleus contains chromosomes that carry the genes
   d how cells divide by mitosis during growth, and by meiosis to produce gametes
   e to relate ways in which animals and plants function as organisms to cell structure and activity.

Humans as organisms

2 Pupils should be taught:

   Nutrition
   a the processes of digestion, including the function of organs and the role of enzymes, stomach acid and biles

   Circulation
   b the structure of the human circulatory system, including the composition and functions of blood
   c that there is an exchange of substances between capillaries and tissues

   Breathing
   d how the structure of the thorax enables ventilation of the lungs

   Respiration
   e that respiration may be either aerobic or anaerobic, depending on the availability of oxygen
   f that an 'oxygen debt' may occur in muscle during vigorous exercise

   Nervous system
   g the pathway taken by impulses in response to a variety of stimuli
   h how the reflex arc makes rapid response to a stimulus possible
   i how the eye functions in response to light

   Hormones
   j the way in which hormonal control occurs, including the effects of insulin and sex hormones
   k some medical uses of hormones, including the control and promotion of fertility and the treatment of diabetes

Double science key stage 4

Sc2 Life processes and living things

Homeostasis
l   the importance of maintaining a constant internal environment
m   how waste products of body functions are removed by the lungs and kidneys
n   how the kidneys regulate the water content of the body
o   how humans maintain a constant body temperature

Health
p   the defence mechanisms of the body, including the role of the skin, blood and mucous membranes of the respiratory tract
q   the effects of solvents, alcohol, tobacco and other drugs on body functions.

Green plants as organisms
3   Pupils should be taught:

Nutrition
a   the reactants in, and products of, photosynthesis
b   that the rate of photosynthesis may be limited by light intensity, carbon dioxide concentration or temperature
c   how the products of photosynthesis are utilised by the plant
d   the importance to healthy plant growth of the uptake and utilisation of mineral salts

Hormones
e   the hormonal control of plant growth and development, including commercial applications

Transport and water relations
f   how plants take up water and transpire
g   the importance of water in the support of plant tissues
h   that substances required for growth and reproduction are transported within plants.

Variation, inheritance and evolution
4   Pupils should be taught:

Variation
a   how variation arises from genetic causes, environmental causes, and a combination of both
b   that sexual reproduction is a source of genetic variation, while asexual reproduction produces clones
c   that mutation is a source of genetic variation and has a number of causes

---

3b → links to other subjects
This requirement builds on Ma4/5c (foundation and higher).

3b → ICT opportunity
Pupils could use dataloggers in investigations of photosynthesis.

3e → ICT opportunity
Pupils could use the internet to find information about commercial applications.

Double science key stage 4

Sc2 Life processes and living things

4h → ICT opportunity
Pupils could use the internet to find out about current developments and issues.

5a → ICT opportunity
Pupils could use spreadsheets to model the effects of competition and predation.

Inheritance

d   how sex is determined in humans
e   the mechanism of monohybrid inheritance where there are dominant and recessive alleles
f   about mechanisms by which some diseases are inherited
g   that the gene is a section of DNA
h   the basic principles of cloning, selective breeding and genetic engineering

Evolution

i   that the fossil record is evidence for evolution
j   how variation and selection may lead to evolution or to extinction.

Living things in their environment

5   Pupils should be taught:

Adaptation and competition

a   how the distribution and relative abundance of organisms in habitats can be explained using ideas of interdependence, adaptation, competition and predation
b   how the impact of humans on the environment depends on social and economic factors, including population size, industrial processes and levels of consumption and waste
c   about the importance of sustainable development

Energy and nutrient transfer

d   how to describe food chains quantitatively using pyramids of biomass
e   how energy is transferred through an ecosystem
f   the role of microbes and other organisms in the decomposition of organic materials and in the cycling of carbon and nitrogen
g   how food production and distribution systems can be managed to improve the efficiency of energy transfers.

Double science key stage 4
Sc3 Materials and their properties

Sc3 Materials and their properties

Classifying materials

1 Pupils should be taught:

   #### Atomic structure
   a that atoms consist of nuclei and electrons
   b the charges and relative masses of protons, neutrons and electrons
   c about mass number, atomic number and isotopes
   d about a model of the way electrons are arranged in atoms
   e how the reactions of elements depend on the arrangement of electrons in their atoms

   #### Bonding
   f that new substances are formed when atoms combine
   g that chemical bonding can be explained in terms of the transfer or sharing of electrons
   h how ions are formed when atoms gain or lose electrons and how giant ionic lattices are held together by the attraction between oppositely charged ions
   i how covalent bonds are formed when atoms share electrons
   j that substances with covalent bonds may form simple molecular structures or giant structures
   k ways in which the physical properties of some substances with giant structures differ from those with simple molecular structures.

Changing materials

2 Pupils should be taught:

   #### Useful products from organic sources
   a how the mixture of substances in crude oil, most of which are hydrocarbons, can be separated by fractional distillation
   b the use of some of the products from crude oil distillation as fuels
   c the products of burning hydrocarbons
   d that alkanes are saturated hydrocarbons, and alkenes are unsaturated hydrocarbons
   e how addition polymers can be formed from the products of crude oil by cracking and polymerisation
   f some uses of addition polymers

1d, 1e → ICT opportunity
Pupils could use software simulations to explore models of the atom and reactions.

2b, 2c, 2f, 2g → ICT opportunity
Pupils could use the internet to find out about products from oil, rocks and minerals and current processes.

Double science key stage 4
Sc3 Materials and their properties

2n, 2o → links to other subjects
These requirements build on Ma2/3n, 4a (foundation) and Ma2/4a (higher).

3 → ICT opportunity
Pupils could use a database of the elements to explore patterns.

Useful products from metal ores and rocks

g about the variety of useful substances [for example, chlorine, sodium hydroxide, glass, cement] that can be made from rocks and minerals

h how the reactivity of a metal affects how it is extracted from its naturally occurring ores

i an example of how a less reactive metal can be extracted by reduction with carbon or carbon monoxide

j an example of how a metal can be purified or recycled by electrolysis

k an example of how a reactive metal can be extracted by electrolysis

Useful products from air

l the importance for agriculture of converting nitrogen to ammonia

m how nitrogenous fertilisers are manufactured, their effect on plant growth, and the environmental consequences of over-use

Quantitative chemistry

n to represent chemical reactions by balanced symbol equations and to use these to predict reacting quantities

o to determine the formulae of simple compounds from reacting masses

Changes to the Earth and atmosphere

p how the Earth's atmosphere and oceans have changed over time

q how the carbon cycle helps to maintain atmospheric composition

r how the sequence of, and evidence for, rock formation and deformation is obtained from the rock record.

Patterns of behaviour

3 Pupils should be taught:

The periodic table

a that there are approximately 100 elements and that all materials are composed of one or more of these

b that the periodic table shows all the elements, arranged in order of ascending atomic number

c the connection between the arrangement of outer electrons and the position of an element in the periodic table

d that elements in the same group of the periodic table have similar properties

e how the properties of elements change gradually from the top to the bottom of a group

f the properties and uses of the noble gases

g the properties and reactions of the alkali metals

h the properties, reactions and uses of the halogens

i about similarities between transition metals and about the characteristic properties of their compounds

j some uses of transition metals

Double science key stage 4
Sc3 Materials and their properties

Chemical reactions

k about different types of chemical reaction, including neutralisation, oxidation, reduction and thermal decomposition, and examples of how these are used to make new materials
l to recognise patterns in chemical reactions and use these to make predictions
m about ways in which knowledge about chemical reactions is applied when new substances are made

Rates of reaction

n about the great variation in the rates at which different reactions take place
o how the rates of reactions can be altered by varying temperature or concentration, or by changing the surface area of a solid reactant, or by adding a catalyst
p how the rates of many reactions depend on the frequency and energy of collisions between particles

Reactions involving enzymes

q about the effect of temperature on the rates of enzyme-catalysed reactions and their dependence on pH
r how enzymes may be used in biotechnology

Reversible reactions

s about manufacturing processes based on reversible reactions, and how the yield of these depends on the conditions

Energy transfer in reactions

t that changes of temperature often accompany reactions
u that reactions can be exothermic or endothermic
v how making and breaking chemical bonds in chemical reactions involves energy transfers.

3n, 3o → ICT opportunity
Pupils could use datalogging to analyse and evaluate reaction data.

3o → links to other subjects
This requirement builds on Ma4/5c (foundation and higher).

3r, 3s → ICT opportunity
Pupils could use the internet to find out about the use of enzymes in biotechnology and other manufacturing processes.

3s → ICT opportunity
Pupils could use simulation software to explore the effects of changing conditions.

Double science key stage 4

Sc4 Physical processes

1c, 1d, 1e → **ICT opportunity**
Pupils could use dataloggers to investigate relationships.

1c, 1e, 1f, 1j, 1o, 2a, 2b, 2d, 2f → **links to other subjects**
These requirements build on Ma2/5f (foundation) and Ma2/5g (higher).

1d → **links to other subjects**
This requirement builds on Ma4/5c (foundation and higher).

2b → **ICT opportunity**
Pupils could use a spreadsheet to analyse data.

Sc4 Physical processes

Electricity

1 Pupils should be taught:

Circuits

a that resistors are heated when charge flows through them
b the qualitative effect of changing resistance on the current in a circuit
c the quantitative relationship between resistance, voltage and current
d how current varies with voltage in a range of devices [for example, resistors, filament bulbs, diodes, light dependent resistors (LDRs) and thermistors]
e that voltage is the energy transferred per unit charge
f the quantitative relationship between power, voltage and current

Mains electricity

g the difference between direct current (dc) and alternating current (ac)
h the functions of the live, neutral and earth wires in the domestic mains supply, and the use of insulation, earthing, fuses and circuit breakers to protect users of electrical equipment
i how electrical heating is used in a variety of ways in domestic contexts
j how measurements of energy transferred are used to calculate the costs of using common domestic appliances

Electric charge

k how an insulating material can be charged by friction
l about forces of attraction between positive and negative charges, and forces of repulsion between like charges
m about common electrostatic phenomena, in terms of the movement of electrons
n the uses and potential dangers of electrostatic charges generated in everyday situations [for example, in photocopiers and inkjet printers]
o the quantitative relationship between steady current, charge and time
p about electric current as the flow of charge carried by free electrons in metals or ions during electrolysis.

Forces and motion

2 Pupils should be taught:

Force and acceleration

a how distance, time and speed can be determined and represented graphically
b about factors affecting vehicle stopping distances
c the difference between speed and velocity
d that acceleration is change in velocity per unit time
e that balanced forces do not alter the velocity of a moving object
f the quantitative relationship between force, mass and acceleration
g that when two bodies interact, the forces they exert on each other are equal and opposite

Double science key stage 4

Sc4 Physical processes

Force and non-uniform motion
h how the forces acting on falling objects change with velocity
i why falling objects may reach a terminal velocity.

Waves

3 Pupils should be taught:

Characteristics of waves
a about the reflection, refraction and diffraction of waves, including light and sound as examples of transverse and longitudinal waves
b the meaning of frequency, wavelength and amplitude of a wave
c the quantitative relationship between the speed, frequency and wavelength of a wave
d that waves transfer energy without transferring matter

The electromagnetic spectrum
e that the electromagnetic spectrum includes radio waves, microwaves, infrared, visible light, ultraviolet waves, X-rays and gamma rays
f some ways in which microwaves, infrared and ultraviolet waves are used and the potential dangers of these
g some uses of X-rays and gamma rays in medicine
h how information can be transmitted along optical fibres
i that radio waves, microwaves, infrared and visible light carry information over large and small distances, including global transmission via satellites
j about ways in which reflection, refraction and diffraction affect communication
k the difference between analogue and digital signals and how more information can be transmitted

Sound and ultrasound
l about sound and ultrasound waves, and some medical and other uses of ultrasound

Seismic waves
m that longitudinal and transverse earthquake waves are transmitted through the Earth, and how their travel times and paths provide evidence for the Earth's layered structure
n that the Earth's outermost layer, the lithosphere, is composed of plates in relative motion, and that plate tectonic processes result in the formation, deformation and recycling of rocks.

2i → ICT opportunity
Pupils could use simulations to investigate falling objects.

3a–3c → ICT opportunity
Pupils could use CD-ROM software to explore wave models.

3c → links to other subjects
This requirement builds on Ma2/5f (foundation) and Ma2/5g (higher).

3n → ICT opportunity
Pupils could use simulation software to model plate tectonic processes.

Double science key stage 4

Sc4 Physical processes

4a, 4b → ICT opportunity
Pupils could use CD-ROM software to simulate movements in the solar system and the universe.

5b → ICT opportunity
Pupils could use the internet to find out about current issues relating to the use of energy sources in Britain and worldwide.

5c–5e, 5i → links to other subjects
These requirements build on Ma2/5f (foundation) and Ma2/5g (higher).

6d → ICT opportunity
Pupils could use simulations to explore half-life.

The Earth and beyond

4   Pupils should be taught:

   The solar system and the wider universe

   a   the relative positions and sizes of planets, stars and other bodies in the universe [for example, comets, meteors, galaxies, black holes]
   b   that gravity acts as a force throughout the universe
   c   how stars evolve over a long timescale
   d   about some ideas used to explain the origin and evolution of the universe
   e   about the search for evidence of life elsewhere in the universe.

Energy resources and energy transfer

5   Pupils should be taught:

   Energy transfer

   a   how insulation is used to reduce transfer of energy from hotter to colder objects
   b   about the efficient use of energy, the need for economical use of energy resources, and the environmental implications of generating energy

   Work, power and energy

   c   the quantitative relationship between force and work
   d   to calculate power in terms of the rate of working or of transferring energy
   e   to calculate kinetic energy and potential energy

   Electromagnetic effects

   f   that a force is exerted on a current-carrying wire in a magnetic field and the application of this effect in simple electric motors
   g   that a voltage is induced when a conductor cuts magnetic field lines and when the magnetic field through a coil changes
   h   how simple ac generators and transformers work
   i   the quantitative relationship between the voltages across the coils in a transformer and the numbers of turns in them
   j   how energy is transferred from power stations to consumers.

Radioactivity

6   Pupils should be taught:

   a   that radioactivity arises from the breakdown of an unstable nucleus
   b   about some sources of the ionising radiation found in all environments
   c   the characteristics of alpha and beta particles and of gamma radiation
   d   the meaning of the term 'half-life'
   e   the beneficial and harmful effects of ionising radiation on matter and living organisms
   f   some uses of radioactivity, including radioactive dating of rocks.

Breadth of study

1 During the key stage, pupils should be taught the **Knowledge, skills and understanding** through:
   a a range of domestic, industrial and environmental contexts
   b considering ways in which science is applied in technological developments
   c considering and evaluating the benefits and drawbacks of scientific and technological developments, including those related to the environment, personal health and quality of life, and those raising ethical issues
   d using a range of sources of information, including ICT-based sources
   e using first-hand and secondary data to carry out a range of scientific investigations, including complete investigations
   f using quantitative approaches, where appropriate, including calculations based on relationships between physical quantities.

2 During the key stage, pupils should be taught to:

   ### Communication
   a use a wide range of scientific, technical and mathematical language, symbols and conventions, including SI units, balanced chemical equations and standard form to communicate ideas and develop an argument

   ### Health and safety
   b recognise that there are hazards in living things, materials and physical processes, and assess risks and take action to reduce risks to themselves and others.

2a → **links to other subjects**
This requirement builds on En1/1e and En3/9b–9d and Ma2/1f (foundation) and Ma2/1h (higher).

General teaching requirements

Inclusion: providing effective learning opportunities for all pupils

Schools have a responsibility to provide a broad and balanced curriculum for all pupils. The National Curriculum is the starting point for planning a school curriculum that meets the specific needs of individuals and groups of pupils. This statutory inclusion statement on providing effective learning opportunities for all pupils outlines how teachers can modify, as necessary, the National Curriculum programmes of study to provide all pupils with relevant and appropriately challenging work at each key stage. It sets out three principles that are essential to developing a more inclusive curriculum:

A Setting suitable learning challenges
B Responding to pupils' diverse learning needs
C Overcoming potential barriers to learning and assessment for individuals and groups of pupils.

Applying these principles should keep to a minimum the need for aspects of the National Curriculum to be disapplied for a pupil.

Schools are able to provide other curricular opportunities outside the National Curriculum to meet the needs of individuals or groups of pupils such as speech and language therapy and mobility training.

Three principles for inclusion

In planning and teaching the National Curriculum, teachers are required to have due regard to the following principles.

A Setting suitable learning challenges

1 Teachers should aim to give every pupil the opportunity to experience success in learning and to achieve as high a standard as possible. The National Curriculum programmes of study set out what most pupils should be taught at each key stage – but teachers should teach the knowledge, skills and understanding in ways that suit their pupils' abilities. This may mean choosing knowledge, skills and understanding from earlier or later key stages so that individual pupils can make progress and show what they can achieve. Where it is appropriate for pupils to make extensive use of content from an earlier key stage, there may not be time to teach all aspects of the age-related programmes of study. A similarly flexible approach will be needed to take account of any gaps in pupils' learning resulting from missed or interrupted schooling [for example, that may be experienced by travellers, refugees, those in care or those with long-term medical conditions, including pupils with neurological problems, such as head injuries, and those with degenerative conditions].

2 For pupils whose attainments fall significantly below the expected levels at a particular key stage, a much greater degree of differentiation will be necessary. In these circumstances, teachers may need to use the content of the programmes of study as a resource or to provide a context, in planning learning appropriate to the age and requirements of their pupils.[1]

3 For pupils whose attainments significantly exceed the expected level of attainment within one or more subjects during a particular key stage, teachers will need to plan suitably challenging work. As well as drawing on materials from later key stages or higher levels of study, teachers may plan further differentiation by extending the breadth and depth of study within individual subjects or by planning work which draws on the content of different subjects.[2]

B Responding to pupils' diverse learning needs

1 When planning, teachers should set high expectations and provide opportunities for all pupils to achieve, including boys and girls, pupils with special educational needs, pupils with disabilities, pupils from all social and cultural backgrounds, pupils of different ethnic groups including travellers, refugees and asylum seekers, and those from diverse linguistic backgrounds. Teachers need to be aware that pupils bring to school different experiences, interests and strengths which will influence the way in which they learn. Teachers should plan their approaches to teaching and learning so that all pupils can take part in lessons fully and effectively.

2 To ensure that they meet the full range of pupils' needs, teachers should be aware of the requirements of the equal opportunities legislation that covers race, gender and disability.[3]

3 Teachers should take specific action to respond to pupils' diverse needs by:
   a creating effective learning environments
   b securing their motivation and concentration
   c providing equality of opportunity through teaching approaches
   d using appropriate assessment approaches
   e setting targets for learning.

Examples for B/3a – creating effective learning environments
Teachers create effective learning environments in which:
- the contribution of all pupils is valued
- all pupils can feel secure and are able to contribute appropriately
- stereotypical views are challenged and pupils learn to appreciate and view positively differences in others, whether arising from race, gender, ability or disability

---

[1] Teachers may find QCA's guidance on planning work for pupils with learning difficulties a helpful companion to the programmes of study.
[2] Teachers may find QCA's guidance on meeting the requirements of gifted and talented pupils a helpful companion to the programmes of study.
[3] The Sex Discrimination Act 1975, the Race Relations Act 1976, the Disability Discrimination Act 1995.

- pupils learn to take responsibility for their actions and behaviours both in school and in the wider community
- all forms of bullying and harassment, including racial harassment, are challenged
- pupils are enabled to participate safely in clothing appropriate to their religious beliefs, particularly in subjects such as science, design and technology and physical education.

Examples for B/3b – securing motivation and concentration

Teachers secure pupils' motivation and concentration by:
- using teaching approaches appropriate to different learning styles
- using, where appropriate, a range of organisational approaches, such as setting, grouping or individual work, to ensure that learning needs are properly addressed
- varying subject content and presentation so that this matches their learning needs
- planning work which builds on their interests and cultural experiences
- planning appropriately challenging work for those whose ability and understanding are in advance of their language skills
- using materials which reflect social and cultural diversity and provide positive images of race, gender and disability
- planning and monitoring the pace of work so that they all have a chance to learn effectively and achieve success
- taking action to maintain interest and continuity of learning for pupils who may be absent for extended periods of time.

Examples for B/3c – providing equality of opportunity

Teaching approaches that provide equality of opportunity include:
- ensuring that boys and girls are able to participate in the same curriculum, particularly in science, design and technology and physical education
- taking account of the interests and concerns of boys and girls by using a range of activities and contexts for work and allowing a variety of interpretations and outcomes, particularly in English, science, design and technology, ICT, art and design, music and physical education
- avoiding gender stereotyping when organising pupils into groups, assigning them to activities or arranging access to equipment, particularly in science, design and technology, ICT, music and physical education
- taking account of pupils' specific religious or cultural beliefs relating to the representation of ideas or experiences or to the use of particular types of equipment, particularly in science, design and technology, ICT and art and design
- enabling the fullest possible participation of pupils with disabilities or particular medical needs in all subjects, offering positive role models and making provision, where necessary, to facilitate access to activities with appropriate support, aids or adaptations. (See **Overcoming potential barriers to learning and assessment for individuals and groups of pupils**.)

Examples for B/3d – using appropriate assessment approaches

Teachers use appropriate assessment approaches that:

- allow for different learning styles and ensure that pupils are given the chance and encouragement to demonstrate their competence and attainment through appropriate means
- are familiar to the pupils and for which they have been adequately prepared
- use materials which are free from discrimination and stereotyping in any form
- provide clear and unambiguous feedback to pupils to aid further learning.

Examples for B/3e – setting targets for learning

Teachers set targets for learning that:

- build on pupils' knowledge, experiences, interests and strengths to improve areas of weakness and demonstrate progression over time
- are attainable and yet challenging and help pupils to develop their self-esteem and confidence in their ability to learn.

C Overcoming potential barriers to learning and assessment for individuals and groups of pupils

A minority of pupils will have particular learning and assessment requirements which go beyond the provisions described in sections A and B and, if not addressed, could create barriers to learning. These requirements are likely to arise as a consequence of a pupil having a special educational need or disability or may be linked to a pupil's progress in learning English as an additional language.

1. Teachers must take account of these requirements and make provision, where necessary, to support individuals or groups of pupils to enable them to participate effectively in the curriculum and assessment activities. During end of key stage assessments, teachers should bear in mind that special arrangements are available to support individual pupils.

Pupils with special educational needs

2. Curriculum planning and assessment for pupils with special educational needs must take account of the type and extent of the difficulty experienced by the pupil. Teachers will encounter a wide range of pupils with special educational needs, some of whom will also have disabilities (see paragraphs C/4 and C/5). In many cases, the action necessary to respond to an individual's requirements for curriculum access will be met through greater differentiation of tasks and materials, consistent with school-based intervention as set out in the SEN Code of Practice. A smaller number of pupils may need access to specialist equipment and approaches or to alternative or adapted activities, consistent with school-based intervention augmented by advice and support from external specialists as described in the SEN Code of Practice, or, in exceptional circumstances, with a statement of special educational need.

Inclusion

Teachers should, where appropriate, work closely with representatives of other agencies who may be supporting the pupil.

3 Teachers should take specific action to provide access to learning for pupils with special educational needs by:
   a providing for pupils who need help with communication, language and literacy
   b planning, where necessary, to develop pupils' understanding through the use of all available senses and experiences
   c planning for pupils' full participation in learning and in physical and practical activities
   d helping pupils to manage their behaviour, to take part in learning effectively and safely, and, at key stage 4, to prepare for work
   e helping individuals to manage their emotions, particularly trauma or stress, and to take part in learning.

Examples for C/3a – helping with communication, language and literacy
Teachers provide for pupils who need help with communication, language and literacy through:
- using texts that pupils can read and understand
- using visual and written materials in different formats, including large print, symbol text and Braille
- using ICT, other technological aids and taped materials
- using alternative and augmentative communication, including signs and symbols
- using translators, communicators and amanuenses.

Examples for C/3b – developing understanding
Teachers develop pupils' understanding through the use of all available senses and experiences, by:
- using materials and resources that pupils can access through sight, touch, sound, taste or smell
- using word descriptions and other stimuli to make up for a lack of first-hand experiences
- using ICT, visual and other materials to increase pupils' knowledge of the wider world
- encouraging pupils to take part in everyday activities such as play, drama, class visits and exploring the environment.

Examples for C/3c – planning for full participation
Teachers plan for pupils' full participation in learning and in physical and practical activities through:
- using specialist aids and equipment
- providing support from adults or peers when needed
- adapting tasks or environments
- providing alternative activities, where necessary.

Inclusion

Examples for C/3d – managing behaviour

Teachers help pupils to manage their behaviour, take part in learning effectively and safely, and, at key stage 4, prepare for work by:
- setting realistic demands and stating them explicitly
- using positive behaviour management, including a clear structure of rewards and sanctions
- giving pupils every chance and encouragement to develop the skills they need to work well with a partner or a group
- teaching pupils to value and respect the contribution of others
- encouraging and teaching independent working skills
- teaching essential safety rules.

Examples for C/3e – managing emotions

Teachers help individuals manage their emotions and take part in learning through:
- identifying aspects of learning in which the pupil will engage and plan short-term, easily achievable goals in selected activities
- providing positive feedback to reinforce and encourage learning and build self-esteem
- selecting tasks and materials sensitively to avoid unnecessary stress for the pupil
- creating a supportive learning environment in which the pupil feels safe and is able to engage with learning
- allowing time for the pupil to engage with learning and gradually increasing the range of activities and demands.

Pupils with disabilities

4   Not all pupils with disabilities will necessarily have special educational needs. Many pupils with disabilities learn alongside their peers with little need for additional resources beyond the aids which they use as part of their daily life, such as a wheelchair, a hearing aid or equipment to aid vision. Teachers must take action, however, in their planning to ensure that these pupils are enabled to participate as fully and effectively as possible within the National Curriculum and the statutory assessment arrangements. Potential areas of difficulty should be identified and addressed at the outset of work, without recourse to the formal provisions for disapplication.

5   Teachers should take specific action to enable the effective participation of pupils with disabilities by:
   a   planning appropriate amounts of time to allow for the satisfactory completion of tasks
   b   planning opportunities, where necessary, for the development of skills in practical aspects of the curriculum
   c   identifying aspects of programmes of study and attainment targets that may present specific difficulties for individuals.

Examples for C/5a – planning to complete tasks

Teachers plan appropriate amounts of time to allow pupils to complete tasks satisfactorily through:

- taking account of the very slow pace at which some pupils will be able to record work, either manually or with specialist equipment, and of the physical effort required
- being aware of the high levels of concentration necessary for some pupils when following or interpreting text or graphics, particularly when using vision aids or tactile methods, and of the tiredness which may result
- allocating sufficient time, opportunity and access to equipment for pupils to gain information through experimental work and detailed observation, including the use of microscopes
- being aware of the effort required by some pupils to follow oral work, whether through use of residual hearing, lip reading or a signer, and of the tiredness or loss of concentration which may occur.

Examples for C/5b – developing skills in practical aspects

Teachers create opportunities for the development of skills in practical aspects of the curriculum through:

- providing adapted, modified or alternative activities or approaches to learning in physical education and ensuring that these have integrity and equivalence to the National Curriculum and enable pupils to make appropriate progress
- providing alternative or adapted activities in science, art and design and design and technology for pupils who are unable to manipulate tools, equipment or materials or who may be allergic to certain types of materials
- ensuring that all pupils can be included and participate safely in geography fieldwork, local studies and visits to museums, historic buildings and sites.

Examples for C/5c – overcoming specific difficulties

Teachers overcome specific difficulties for individuals presented by aspects of the programmes of study and attainment targets through:

- using approaches to enable hearing impaired pupils to learn about sound in science and music
- helping visually impaired pupils to learn about light in science, to access maps and visual resources in geography and to evaluate different products in design and technology and images in art and design
- providing opportunities for pupils to develop strength in depth where they cannot meet the particular requirements of a subject, such as the visual requirements in art and design and the singing requirements in music
- discounting these aspects in appropriate individual cases when required to make a judgement against level descriptions.

Pupils who are learning English as an additional language

6   Pupils for whom English is an additional language have diverse needs in terms of support necessary in English language learning. Planning should take account of such factors as the pupil's age, length of time in this country, previous educational experience and skills in other languages. Careful monitoring of each pupil's progress in the acquisition of English language skills and of subject knowledge and understanding will be necessary to confirm that no learning difficulties are present.

7   The ability of pupils for whom English is an additional language to take part in the National Curriculum may be ahead of their communication skills in English. Teachers should plan learning opportunities to help pupils develop their English and should aim to provide the support pupils need to take part in all subject areas.

8   Teachers should take specific action to help pupils who are learning English as an additional language by:
    a   developing their spoken and written English
    b   ensuring access to the curriculum and to assessment.

Examples for C/8a – developing spoken and written English
Teachers develop pupils' spoken and written English through:
- ensuring that vocabulary work covers both the technical and everyday meaning of key words, metaphors and idioms
- explaining clearly how speaking and writing in English are structured to achieve different purposes, across a range of subjects
- providing a variety of reading material [for example, pupils' own work, the media, ICT, literature, reference books] that highlight the different ways English is used, especially those that help pupils to understand society and culture
- ensuring that there are effective opportunities for talk and that talk is used to support writing in all subjects
- where appropriate, encouraging pupils to transfer their knowledge, skills and understanding of one language to another, pointing out similarities and differences between languages
- building on pupils' experiences of language at home and in the wider community, so that their developing uses of English and other languages support one another.

Examples for C/8b – ensuring access
Teachers make sure pupils have access to the curriculum and to assessment through:
- using accessible texts and materials that suit pupils' ages and levels of learning
- providing support by using ICT or video or audio materials, dictionaries and translators, readers and amanuenses
- using home or first language, where appropriate.

Inclusion

Additional information for science

Teachers may find the following additional information helpful when implementing the statutory inclusion statement: **Providing effective learning opportunities for all pupils.** Teachers need to consider the full requirements of the inclusion statement when planning for individuals or groups of pupils. There are specific references to science in the examples for B/3a, B/3c, C/5a, C/5b and C/5c.

To overcome any potential barriers to learning in science, some pupils may require:
- support to overcome difficulties with mobility or manipulative skills so that they can participate as fully and as safely as possible in experimental work. Support could be provided [for example, by adapting or using alternative activities, adapting equipment or by using specialist items, including ICT, or providing adult or peer support]
- additional time to compensate for difficulties in managing visual information, particularly when making observations and accessing information in experimental work or through the use of microscopes
- support in lessons about light so that despite their visual impairment pupils are able to gain as much access as possible to the activities [for example, by use of ICT, by using their knowledge that many light sources produce heat]
- support in lessons about sounds so that despite their hearing impairment pupils are able to gain as much access as possible to activities [for example, by the use of oscilloscopes and sound level meters to provide visual demonstrations].

In assessment:
- pupils who are unable to use equipment and materials, including those who are visually or hearing impaired, may be unable to achieve certain aspects of the level descriptions. When a judgement against level descriptions is required, assessment of progress should discount these identified aspects.

Use of language across the curriculum

1. Pupils should be taught in all subjects to express themselves correctly and appropriately and to read accurately and with understanding. Since standard English, spoken and written, is the predominant language in which knowledge and skills are taught and learned, pupils should be taught to recognise and use standard English.

Writing

2. In writing, pupils should be taught to use correct spelling and punctuation and follow grammatical conventions. They should also be taught to organise their writing in logical and coherent forms.

Speaking

3. In speaking, pupils should be taught to use language precisely and cogently.

Listening

4. Pupils should be taught to listen to others, and to respond and build on their ideas and views constructively.

Reading

5. In reading, pupils should be taught strategies to help them read with understanding, to locate and use information, to follow a process or argument and summarise, and to synthesise and adapt what they learn from their reading.

6. Pupils should be taught the technical and specialist vocabulary of subjects and how to use and spell these words. They should also be taught to use the patterns of language vital to understanding and expression in different subjects. These include the construction of sentences, paragraphs and texts that are often used in a subject [for example, language to express causality, chronology, logic, exploration, hypothesis, comparison, and how to ask questions and develop arguments].

Use of information and communication technology across the curriculum

1 Pupils should be given opportunities[1] to apply and develop their ICT capability through the use of ICT tools to support their learning in all subjects (with the exception of physical education at key stages 1 and 2).

2 Pupils should be given opportunities to support their work by being taught to:
 a find things out from a variety of sources, selecting and synthesising the information to meet their needs and developing an ability to question its accuracy, bias and plausibility
 b develop their ideas using ICT tools to amend and refine their work and enhance its quality and accuracy
 c exchange and share information, both directly and through electronic media
 d review, modify and evaluate their work, reflecting critically on its quality, as it progresses.

---

[1] At key stage 1, there are no statutory requirements to teach the use of ICT in the programmes of study for the non-core foundation subjects. Teachers should use their judgement to decide where it is appropriate to teach the use of ICT across these subjects at key stage 1. At other key stages, there are statutory requirements to use ICT in all subjects, except physical education.

Health and safety

1. This statement applies to science, design and technology, information and communication technology, art and design, and physical education.

2. When working with tools, equipment and materials, in practical activities and in different environments, including those that are unfamiliar, pupils should be taught:
   a. about hazards, risks and risk control
   b. to recognise hazards, assess consequent risks and take steps to control the risks to themselves and others
   c. to use information to assess the immediate and cumulative risks
   d. to manage their environment to ensure the health and safety of themselves and others
   e. to explain the steps they take to control risks.

The attainment targets for science

Science levels

Sc1 Scientific enquiry

About the attainment targets

An attainment target sets out the 'knowledge, skills and understanding that pupils of different abilities and maturities are expected to have by the end of each key stage'[1]. Except in the case of citizenship[2], attainment targets consist of eight level descriptions of increasing difficulty, plus a description for exceptional performance above level 8. Each level description describes the types and range of performance that pupils working at that level should characteristically demonstrate.

The level descriptions provide the basis for making judgements about pupils' performance at the end of key stages 1, 2 and 3. At key stage 4, national qualifications are the main means of assessing attainment in science.

Range of levels within which the great majority of pupils are expected to work		Expected attainment for the majority of pupils at the end of the key stage	
Key stage 1	1–3	at age 7	2
Key stage 2	2–5	at age 11	4
Key stage 3	3–7	at age 14	5/6[3]

Assessing attainment at the end of a key stage

In deciding on a pupil's level of attainment at the end of a key stage, teachers should judge which description best fits the pupil's performance. When doing so, each description should be considered alongside descriptions for adjacent levels.

Arrangements for statutory assessment at the end of each key stage are set out in detail in QCA's annual booklets about assessment and reporting arrangements.

Examples in the level descriptions

The examples in grey type are not statutory.

---

[1] As defined by the Education Act 1996, section 353a.
[2] In citizenship, expected performance for the majority of pupils at the end of key stages 3 and 4 is set out in end of key stage descriptions.
[3] Including modern foreign languages.

Science levels
Sc1 Scientific enquiry

Level 6
Pupils describe evidence for some accepted scientific ideas and explain how the interpretation of evidence by scientists leads to the development and acceptance of new ideas. In their own investigative work, they use scientific knowledge and understanding to identify an appropriate approach. They select and use sources of information effectively. They make enough measurements, comparisons and observations for the task. They measure a variety of quantities with precision, using instruments with fine-scale divisions. They choose scales for graphs and diagrams that enable them to show data and features effectively. They identify measurements and observations that do not fit the main pattern shown. They draw conclusions that are consistent with the evidence and use scientific knowledge and understanding to explain them. They make reasoned suggestions about how their working methods could be improved. They select and use appropriate methods for communicating qualitative and quantitative data using scientific language and conventions.

Level 7
Pupils describe some predictions based on scientific theories and give examples of the evidence collected to test these predictions. In their own work, they use scientific knowledge and understanding to decide on appropriate approaches to questions. They identify the key factors in complex contexts and in contexts in which variables cannot readily be controlled, and plan appropriate procedures. They synthesise information from a range of sources, and identify possible limitations in secondary data. They make systematic observations and measurements with precision, using a wide range of apparatus. They identify when they need to repeat measurements, comparisons and observations in order to obtain reliable data. Where appropriate, they represent data in graphs, using lines of best fit. They draw conclusions that are consistent with the evidence and explain these using scientific knowledge and understanding. They begin to consider whether the data they have collected are sufficient for the conclusions they have drawn. They communicate what they have done using a wide range of scientific and technical language and conventions, including symbols and flow diagrams.

Level 8
Pupils give examples of scientific explanations or models that have had to be changed in the light of additional scientific evidence. They evaluate and synthesise data from a range of sources. They recognise that investigating different kinds of scientific questions requires different strategies, and use scientific knowledge and understanding to select an appropriate strategy in their own work. They decide which observations are relevant in qualitative work and include suitable detail in their records. They decide the level of precision needed in comparisons or measurements, and collect data enabling them to test relationships between variables. They identify and begin to explain anomalous observations and measurements and allow for these when they draw graphs. They use scientific knowledge and understanding to draw conclusions from their evidence. They consider graphs and tables of results critically. They communicate findings and arguments using appropriate scientific language and conventions, showing awareness of a range of views.

Exceptional performance
Pupils give examples of scientific explanations and models that have been challenged by subsequent experiments and explain the significance of the evidence in modifying scientific theories. They evaluate and synthesise data from a range of sources. They recognise that investigating different kinds of scientific questions requires different strategies, and use scientific knowledge and understanding to select an appropriate strategy in their own work. They make records of relevant observations and comparisons, clearly identifying points of particular significance. They decide the level of precision needed in measurements and collect data that satisfy these requirements. They use their data to test relationships between variables. They identify and explain anomalous observations and measurements, allowing for these when they draw graphs. They use scientific knowledge and understanding to interpret trends and patterns and to draw conclusions from their evidence. They consider graphs and tables of results critically and give reasoned accounts of how they could collect additional evidence. They communicate findings and arguments using appropriate scientific language and conventions, showing their awareness of the degree of uncertainty and a range of alternative views.

Attainment target 1: scientific enquiry

Level 1
Pupils describe or respond appropriately to simple features of objects, living things and events they observe, communicating their findings in simple ways [for example, talking about their work, through drawings, simple charts].

Level 2
Pupils respond to suggestions about how to find things out and, with help, make their own suggestions about how to collect data to answer questions. They use simple texts, with help, to find information. They use simple equipment provided and make observations related to their task. They observe and compare objects, living things and events. They describe their observations using scientific vocabulary and record them, using simple tables when appropriate. They say whether what happened was what they expected.

Level 3
Pupils respond to suggestions and put forward their own ideas about how to find the answer to a question. They recognise why it is important to collect data to answer questions. They use simple texts to find information. They make relevant observations and measure quantities, such as length or mass, using a range of simple equipment. Where appropriate, they carry out a fair test with some help, recognising and explaining why it is fair. They record their observations in a variety of ways. They provide explanations for observations and for simple patterns in recorded measurements. They communicate in a scientific way what they have found out and suggest improvements in their work.

Level 4
Pupils recognise that scientific ideas are based on evidence. In their own investigative work, they decide on an appropriate approach [for example, using a fair test] to answer a question. Where appropriate, they describe, or show in the way they perform their task, how to vary one factor while keeping others the same. Where appropriate, they make predictions. They select information from sources provided for them. They select suitable equipment and make a series of observations and measurements that are adequate for the task. They record their observations, comparisons and measurements using tables and bar charts. They begin to plot points to form simple graphs, and use these graphs to point out and interpret patterns in their data. They begin to relate their conclusions to these patterns and to scientific knowledge and understanding, and to communicate them with appropriate scientific language. They suggest improvements in their work, giving reasons.

Level 5
Pupils describe how experimental evidence and creative thinking have been combined to provide a scientific explanation [for example, Jenner's work on vaccination at key stage 2, Lavoisier's work on burning at key stage 3]. When they try to answer a scientific question, they identify an appropriate approach. They select from a range of sources of information. When the investigation involves a fair test, they identify key factors to be considered. Where appropriate, they make predictions based on their scientific knowledge and understanding. They select apparatus for a range of tasks and plan to use it effectively. They make a series of observations, comparisons or measurements with precision appropriate to the task. They begin to repeat observations and measurements and to offer simple explanations for any differences they encounter. They record observations and measurements systematically and, where appropriate, present data as line graphs. They draw conclusions that are consistent with the evidence and begin to relate these to scientific knowledge and understanding. They make practical suggestions about how their working methods could be improved. They use appropriate scientific language and conventions to communicate quantitative and qualitative data.

Science levels

Sc2 Life processes and living things

Science levels
Sc2 Life processes and living things

Level 5
Pupils demonstrate an increasing knowledge and understanding of life processes and living things drawn from the key stage 2 or key stage 3 programme of study. They describe the main functions of organs of the human body [for example, the heart at key stage 2, stomach at key stage 3], and of the plant [for example, the stamen at key stage 2, root hairs at key stage 3]. They explain how these functions are essential to the organism. They describe the main stages of the life cycles of humans and flowering plants and point out similarities. They recognise that there is a great variety of living things and understand the importance of classification. They explain that different organisms are found in different habitats because of differences in environmental factors [for example, the availability of light or water].

Level 6
Pupils use knowledge and understanding drawn from the key stage 3 programme of study to describe and explain life processes and features of living things. They use appropriate scientific terminology when they describe life processes [for example, respiration, photosynthesis] in animals and plants. They distinguish between related processes [for example, pollination, fertilisation]. They describe simple cell structure and identify differences between simple animal and plant cells. They describe some of the causes of variation between living things. They explain that the distribution and abundance of organisms in habitats are affected by environmental factors [for example, the availability of light or water].

Level 7
Pupils use knowledge and understanding of life processes and living things drawn from the key stage 3 programme of study to make links between life processes in animals and plants and the organ systems involved. They explain the processes of respiration and photosynthesis in terms of the main underlying chemical change. They use their knowledge of cell structure to explain how cells [for example, ovum, sperm, root hair] are adapted to their functions. They identify common variations between individuals, including some features [for example, eye colour] that are inherited and others [for example, height] that can also be affected by environmental factors. They construct models [for example, food webs, pyramids of numbers] to show feeding relationships, and explain how these relationships affect population size.

Level 8
Pupils demonstrate an extensive knowledge and understanding of life processes and living things drawn from the key stage 3 programme of study by describing and explaining how biological systems function. They relate the cellular structure of organs to the associated life processes [for example, the absorption of food in the digestive system, gas exchange in the lungs]. They recognise, predict and explain changes in biological systems [for example, the effect of increased carbon dioxide concentration on the growth of greenhouse crops, the consequences of smoking for organ systems]. They explain how characteristics can be inherited by individuals and apply their knowledge [for example, in relation to selective breeding]. They predict the short-term and long-term effects of environmental change on ecosystems and use their understanding of such systems to justify their predictions.

Exceptional performance
Pupils demonstrate both breadth and depth of knowledge and understanding drawn from the key stage 3 programme of study when they describe and explain how biological systems function. They recognise that organisms respond to change, and describe ways in which this is achieved. They relate their understanding of internal and external cellular structures to life processes [for example, the increased surface areas of cells in the digestive system]. They relate their understanding of cellular structure to inheritance and variation and explain how this leads to new varieties [for example, how genetic engineering is a modern form of selective breeding]. They recognise the importance of quantitative data [for example, related to populations in an environment] when they describe and explain patterns of change within an ecosystem.

Attainment target 2: life processes and living things

Level 1
Pupils recognise and name external parts of the body [for example, head, arm] and of plants [for example, leaf, flower]. They communicate observations of a range of animals and plants in terms of features [for example, colour of coat, size of leaf]. They recognise and identify a range of common animals [for example, fly, goldfish, robin].

Level 2
Pupils use their knowledge about living things to describe the basic conditions [for example, a supply of food, water, air, light] that animals and plants need in order to survive. They recognise that living things grow and reproduce. They sort living things into groups, using simple features. They describe the basis for their groupings [for example, number of legs, shape of leaf]. They recognise that different living things are found in different places [for example, ponds, woods].

Level 3
Pupils use their knowledge and understanding of basic life processes [for example, growth, reproduction] when they describe differences between living and non-living things. They provide simple explanations for changes in living things [for example, diet affecting the health of humans or other animals, lack of light or water altering plant growth]. They identify ways in which an animal is suited to its environment [for example, a fish having fins to help it swim].

Level 4
Pupils demonstrate knowledge and understanding of life processes and living things drawn from the key stage 2 or key stage 3 programme of study. They use scientific names for some major organs of body systems [for example, the heart at key stage 2, the stomach at key stage 3] and identify the position of these organs in the human body. They identify organs [for example, stamen at key stage 2, stigma, root hairs at key stage 3] of different plants they observe. They use keys based on observable external features to help them to identify and group living things systematically. They recognise that feeding relationships exist between plants and animals in a habitat, and describe these relationships using food chains and terms [for example, predator and prey].

Science levels

Sc3 Materials and their properties

Science levels

Sc3 Materials and their properties

Level 5
Pupils demonstrate an increasing knowledge and understanding of materials and their properties drawn from the key stage 2 or key stage 3 programme of study. They describe some metallic properties [for example, good electrical conductivity] and use these properties to distinguish metals from other solids. They identify a range of contexts in which changes [for example, evaporation, condensation] take place. They use knowledge about how a specific mixture [for example, salt and water, sand and water] can be separated to suggest ways in which other similar mixtures might be separated.

Level 6
Pupils use knowledge and understanding of the nature and behaviour of materials drawn from the key stage 3 programme of study to describe chemical and physical changes, and how new materials can be made. They recognise that matter is made up of particles, and describe differences between the arrangement and movement of particles in solids, liquids and gases. They identify and describe similarities between some chemical reactions [for example, the reactions of acids with metals, the reactions of a variety of substances with oxygen]. They use word equations to summarise simple reactions. They relate changes of state to energy transfers in a range of contexts [for example, the formation of igneous rocks].

Level 7
Pupils use knowledge and understanding drawn from the key stage 3 programme of study to make links between the nature and behaviour of materials and the particles of which they are composed. They use the particle model of matter in explanations of phenomena [for example, changes of state]. They explain differences between elements, compounds and mixtures in terms of their constituent particles. They recognise that elements and compounds can be represented by symbols and formulae. They apply their knowledge of physical and chemical processes to explain the behaviour of materials in a variety of contexts [for example, the way in which natural limestone is changed through the action of rainwater, ways in which rocks are weathered]. They use patterns of reactivity [for example, those associated with a reactivity series of metals] to make predictions about other chemical reactions.

Level 8
Pupils demonstrate an extensive knowledge and understanding drawn from the key stage 3 programme of study, which they use to describe and explain the behaviour of, and changes to, materials. They use the particle model in a wide range of contexts. They describe what happens in a range of chemical reactions and classify some [for example, oxidation, neutralisation]. They represent common compounds by chemical formulae and use these formulae to form balanced symbol equations for reactions [for example, those of acids with metals, carbonates or oxides]. They apply their knowledge of patterns in chemical reactions to suggest how substances [for example, salts] could be made.

Exceptional performance
Pupils demonstrate both breadth and depth of knowledge and understanding drawn from the key stage 3 programme of study when they describe and explain the nature and behaviour of materials. They use particle theory in a wider range of contexts, recognising that differences in the properties of materials relate to the nature of the particles within them. They recognise, and give explanations for, examples of chemical behaviour that do not fit expected patterns. They routinely use balanced symbol equations for reactions. They interpret quantitative data about chemical reactions, suggesting explanations for patterns identified.

Attainment target 3: materials and their properties

Level 1
Pupils know about a range of properties [for example, texture, appearance] and communicate observations of materials in terms of these properties.

Level 2
Pupils identify a range of common materials and know about some of their properties. They describe similarities and differences between materials. They sort materials into groups and describe the basis for their groupings in everyday terms [for example, shininess, hardness, smoothness]. They describe ways in which some materials are changed by heating or cooling or by processes such as bending or stretching.

Level 3
Pupils use their knowledge and understanding of materials when they describe a variety of ways of sorting them into groups according to their properties. They explain simply why some materials are particularly suitable for specific purposes [for example, glass for windows, copper for electrical cables]. They recognise that some changes [for example, the freezing of water] can be reversed and some [for example, the baking of clay] cannot, and they classify changes in this way.

Level 4
Pupils demonstrate knowledge and understanding of materials and their properties drawn from the key stage 2 or key stage 3 programme of study. They describe differences between the properties of different materials and explain how these differences are used to classify substances [for example, as solids, liquids, gases at key stage 2, as acids, alkalis at key stage 3]. They describe some methods [for example, filtration, distillation] that are used to separate simple mixtures. They use scientific terms [for example, evaporation, condensation] to describe changes. They use knowledge about some reversible and irreversible changes to make simple predictions about whether other changes are reversible or not.

Science levels

Sc4 Physical processes

Science levels

Sc4 Physical processes

Level 5
Pupils demonstrate knowledge and understanding of physical processes drawn from the key stage 2 or key stage 3 programme of study. They use ideas to explain how to make a range of changes [for example, altering the current in a circuit, altering the pitch or loudness of a sound]. They use some abstract ideas in descriptions of familiar phenomena [for example, objects are seen when light from them enters the eye at key stage 2, forces are balanced when an object is stationary at key stage 3]. They use simple models to explain effects that are caused by the movement of the Earth [for example, the length of a day or year].

Level 6
Pupils use and apply knowledge and understanding of physical processes drawn from the key stage 3 programme of study. They use abstract ideas in some descriptions and explanations [for example, electric current as a way of transferring energy, the sum of several forces determining changes in the direction or the speed of movement of an object, wind and waves as energy resources available for use]. They recognise, and can give examples of, the wide application of many physical concepts [for example, the transfer of energy by light, sound or electricity, the refraction and dispersion of light]. They give explanations of phenomena in which a number of factors have to be considered [for example, the relative brightness of planets and stars].

Level 7
Pupils use knowledge and understanding of physical processes drawn from the key stage 3 programme of study to make links between different phenomena. They make connections between electricity and magnetism when explaining phenomena [for example, the strength of electromagnets]. They use some quantitative definitions [for example, speed, pressure] and perform calculations, using the correct units. They apply abstract ideas in explanations of a range of physical phenomena [for example, the appearance of objects in different colours of light, the relationship between the frequency of vibration and the pitch of a sound, the role of gravitational attraction in determining the motion of bodies in the solar system, the dissipation of energy during energy transfers].

Level 8
Pupils demonstrate an extensive knowledge and understanding of the physical processes in the key stage 3 programme of study. They use models to describe and explain phenomena [for example, the magnetic field of an electromagnet, the passage of sound waves through a medium]. They use quantitative relationships between physical quantities in calculations that may involve more than one step. They offer detailed and sometimes quantitative interpretations of graphs [for example, speed–time graphs]. They consider ways of obtaining data [for example, of the solar system] and they use their knowledge of physical processes to explain patterns that they find. They consider physical phenomena from different perspectives [for example, relating the dissipation of energy during energy transfer to the need to conserve limited energy resources].

Exceptional performance
Pupils demonstrate both breadth and depth of knowledge and understanding of the physical processes in the key stage 3 programme of study when they describe and explain physical phenomena. They make effective use of a range of quantitative relationships between physical quantities. They understand how models [for example, the particle model] are useful in explaining physical phenomena [for example, how sweating causes cooling]. They apply their understanding of physical phenomena to a wide range of systems [for example, recognising the role of gravitational attraction in determining the movement of satellites, planets and stars]. They recognise the importance of quantitative data and make effective use of this when they consider questions such as energy efficiency.

Attainment target 4: physical processes

Level 1
Pupils communicate observations of changes in light, sound or movement that result from actions [for example, switching on a simple electrical circuit, pushing and pulling objects]. They recognise that sound and light come from a variety of sources and name some of these.

Level 2
Pupils know about a range of physical phenomena and recognise and describe similarities and differences associated with them. They compare the way in which devices [for example, bulbs] work in different electrical circuits. They compare the brightness or colour of lights, and the loudness or pitch of sounds. They compare the movement of different objects in terms of speed or direction.

Level 3
Pupils use their knowledge and understanding of physical phenomena to link cause and effect in simple explanations [for example, a bulb failing to light because of a break in an electrical circuit, the direction or speed of movement of an object changing because of a push or a pull]. They begin to make simple generalisations about physical phenomena [for example, explaining that sounds they hear become fainter the further they are from the source].

Level 4
Pupils demonstrate knowledge and understanding of physical processes drawn from the key stage 2 or key stage 3 programme of study. They describe and explain physical phenomena [for example, how a particular device may be connected to work in an electrical circuit, how the apparent position of the Sun changes over the course of a day]. They make generalisations about physical phenomena [for example, motion is affected by forces, including gravitational attraction, magnetic attraction and friction]. They use physical ideas to explain simple phenomena [for example, the formation of shadows, sounds being heard through a variety of materials].

Notes

Mixtures and colours

Homework H5

1 Look at the chromatogram below.

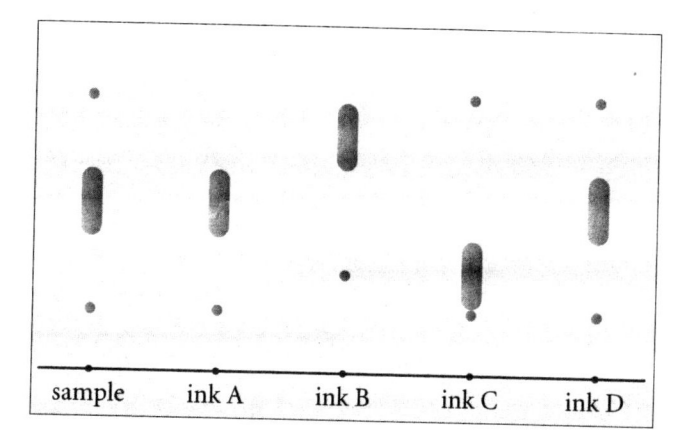

a Which ink (A, B, C or D) is present in the ink sample from the pen.

b Explain your answer to **a**.

c How might chromatography be useful to the police if they were investigating who sent some handwritten threatening letters?

2 Use the chromatogram above to draw, as accurately as possible:

a The chromatogram you would get from a mixture of ink **A** and ink **B**.

b The chromatogram you would get from a mixture of ink **C** and ink **D**.

c The chromatogram you would get from a mixture of ink **B** and ink **D**.

3 Why might the chromatogram from a mixture of ink **B** with ink **C** be confusing?

© I Bradley, C Tear, M Winterbottom, S Young, 2001, The Heinemann Science Scheme

Acknowledgements

About the work used in this document
The artwork and photographs used in this book are the result of a national selection organised by QCA and the Design Council. We would like to thank all 3,108 pupils who took part and especially the following pupils and schools whose work has been used throughout the National Curriculum.

Pupils Frankie Allen, Sarah Anderson, Naomi Ball, Kristina Battleday, Ashley Boyle, Martin Broom, Katie Brown, Alex Bryant, Tania Burnett, Elizabeth Burrows, Caitie Calloway, Kavandeep Chahal, Donna Clarke, Leah Cliffe, Megan Coombs, Andrew Cornford, Samantha Davidoff, Jodie Evans, Holly Fowler, Rachel Fort, Christopher Fort, Hannah Foster, Ruth Fry, Nicholas Furlonge, Tasleem Ghanchi, Rebecca Goodwin, Megan Goodwin, Joanna Gray, Alisha Grazette, Emma Habbeshon, Zoe Hall, Kay Hampshire, Jessica Harris, Aimee Howard, Amy Hurst, Katherine Hymers, Safwan Ismael, Tamaszina Jacobs-Abiola, Tomi Johnson, Richard Jones, Bruno Jones, Thomas Kelleher, Sophie Lambert, Gareth Lloyd, Ope Majekodunmi, Sophie Manchester, Alex Massie, Amy McNair, Dale Meachen, Katherine Mills, Rebecca Moore, Andrew Morgan, Amber Murrell, Sally O'Connor, Rosie O'Reilly, Antonia Pain, Daniel Pamment, Jennie Plant, Christopher Prest, Megan Ramsay, Alice Ross, David Rowles, Amy Sandford, Zeba Saudagar, Nathan Scarfe, Daniel Scully, Bilal Shakoor, Sandeep Sharma, Morrad Siyahla, Daryl Smith, Catriona Statham, Scott Taylor, Amy Thornton, Jessica Tidmarsh, Alix Tinkler, Lucy Titford, Marion Tulloch, Charlotte Ward, Kaltuun Warsame, Emily Webb, Bradley West, Daniel Wilkinson, Soriah Williams, Susan Williamson, Helen Williamson, Charlotte Windmill, Ryan Wollan, Olivia Wright.

Schools Adam's Grammar School, Almondbury Junior School, Bishops Castle Community College, Bolton Brow Junior and Infant School, Boxford C of E Voluntary Controlled Primary School, Bugbrooke School, Cantell School, Charnwood Primary School, Cheselbourne County First School, Chester Catholic High School, Dales Infant School, Deanery C of E High School, Driffield C of E Infants' School, Dursley Primary School, Fourfields County Primary School, Furze Infants School, Gosforth High School, Grahame Park Junior School, Green Park Combined School, Gusford Community Primary School, Hartshill School, Headington School, Holyport Manor School, Jersey College for Girls Preparatory School, King Edward VI School, King James's School, Kingsway Junior School, Knutsford High School, Leiston Primary School, Maltby Manor Infant School, Mullion Comprehensive School, North Marston C of E First School, Norton Hill School, Penglais School, Priory Secondary School, Redknock School, Richard Whittington Primary School, Ringwood School, Sarah Bonnell School, Sedgemoor Manor Infants School, Selly Park Technology College for Girls, Southwark Infant School, St Albans High School for Girls, St Denys C of E Infant School, St Helen's C of E (Aided) Primary School, St John's Infants School, St Joseph's RC Infant School, St Laurence School, St Mary Magdalene School, St Matthews C of E Aided Primary School, St Michael's C of E School, St Saviour's and St Olave's School, St Thomas The Martyr C of E Primary School, Sawtry Community College, The Duchess's High School, Tideway School, Torfield School, Trinity C of E Primary School, Upper Poppelton School, Walton High School.

QCA and the Design Council would also like to thank the figures from public life who contributed their ideas about the value of each curriculum subject.

Mixtures and colours

Homework

H5

1 Look at the chromatogram below.

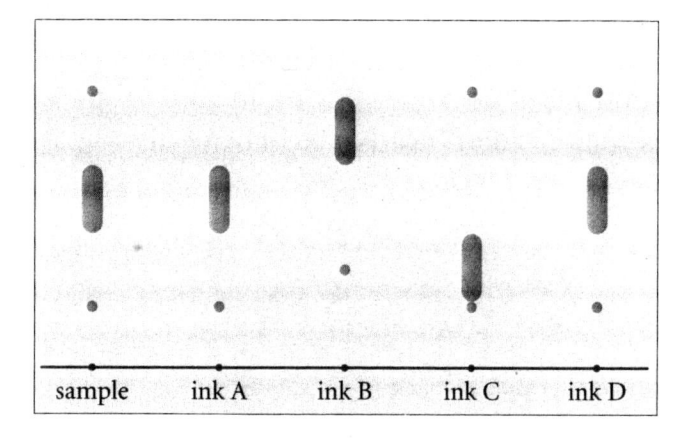

a Which ink (A, B, C or D) is present in the ink sample from the pen.
b Explain your answer to **a**.
c How might chromatography be useful to the police if they were investigating who sent some handwritten threatening letters?

2 Use the chromatogram above to draw, as accurately as possible:
   a The chromatogram you would get from a mixture of ink **A** and ink **B**.
   b The chromatogram you would get from a mixture of ink **C** and ink **D**.
   c The chromatogram you would get from a mixture of ink **B** and ink **D**.

3 Why might the chromatogram from a mixture of ink **B** with ink **C** be confusing?

Ink is a mixture not a compound.

① Why use pencil?

② What happens to the water level on the paper.

③ Observations

④ O

Notes